AGILE DEVOPS Self-Assessment Maturity Model

By
Sudipta Malakar

Acknowledgement

No task is a single man's effort. Cooperation and Coordination of various people at different levels go into successful implementation of this book.

There is always a sense of gratitude, which everyone expresses others for their helpful and needy services they render during difficult phases of life and to achieve the goal already set.
At the outset I am thankful to the almighty that is constantly and invisibly guiding everybody and have also helped me to work on the right path.

I am son of Retired Professor (*Shri Ganesh Chandra Malakar*). I am indebted to my Father as without his support it was not possible to reach this Milestone. My loving mother (*Smt. Sikha Malakar*) always provides inspiration to me. My cute loving Son (*Master Shreyan Malakar*) is always providing me precious support at his level best.

I am thankful to my parents, spouse, son, family and Sirs (Mike Cohn, CST, Nanda Lankalapalli CST, Peter Stevens, CST, Abid Quereshi, CST) for their guidance which motivated me to work for the betterment of consultants by writing the book with sincerity and honesty. Without their support, this book was not possible.

Finally, I thank everyone who has directly or indirectly contributed to complete this authentic work.

PREFACE

For decades, technology and business leaders have struggled to balance agility, reliability, automation and security, and the consequences of failure are always significant. The effective management of technology is critical for business competitiveness. High-performing organizations are 2.5 times more likely to exceed profitability, market share, and productivity goals. The Agile & DevOps handbook shows leaders how to create the cultural norms and the technical best practices necessary to maximize organizational learning, increase employee satisfaction, win in the marketplace, enhance Customer / business delight and capture new business.

If you are a tech developer, IT Consultant, Agile Coach, Scrum Master, Product Owner, Leader, Manager, Sr. Manager, part of product management team or IT operator, then this book is perfect for you in order to increase profitability, exceed productivity goals and elevate work culture through Agile & DevOps methodology. So if you want to know what the basic principles of Agile & DevOps movement are and how to incorporate Agile & DevOps concept and practices into your own organization. This book will guide you through the world of the Agile & DevOps and through its main principles so you can greatly increase organizational potential and reduce the risk of failure. Learn why all major organizations are adopting the Agile & DevOps methodology and follow their success story with Agile & DevOps.

John Willis says - If you can't measure you can't improve. A successful DevOps implementation will measure everything it can as often as it can… performance metrics, process metrics and even people metrics.

The examples given in book are user-focused and have been highly updated including topics, figures, strategies, best practices and real-life examples, demos and case studies.

All the tools you need to an in-depth DevOps Self-Assessment Maturity model. Featuring 100 PLUS new and updated case-based questions, organized into seven core areas of process design, this Self-Assessment will help you identify areas in which DevOps improvements can be made.

This book promises to be a very good starting point for beginners and an asset for those having insight towards Agile, DevOps, Testing Automation and Technical best practices.

It is said **"To err is human, to forgive divine"**. Although the book is written with sincerity and honesty but in this light, I wish that the shortcomings of the book will be forgiven. At the same the author is open to any kind of constructive criticisms and suggestions for further improvement. All intelligent suggestions are welcome and the author will try their best to incorporate such in valuable suggestions in the subsequent editions of this book.

Table of Contents

Chapter 1 - Agile Introduction 11
   1.1. Agile manifesto and key agile principles 11
      1.1.1. Agile manifesto 11
      1.1.2. Agile principles 12
      1.1.3. Key agile principles 12
   1.2. Agile Values 12
   1.3. Traditional life cycle versus Agile development 13
   1.4. AGILITY VERSUS AGILE 14
   1.5. The State of Agility 14
   1.6. Three Steps to increase Agility 16
   1.7. Agile Framework 17
   1.8. Agile Concepts 18
   1.9. Benefits of Agile 18
   2.0. Technical best practices 19
   2.1. Test driven development 19
   2.2. Advantages of test driven development 19
   2.3. Tools of Test driven development 20
   2.4. Code refactoring 20
   2.4.1 Techniques of Code refactoring 20
      A. Increasing level of abstraction 20
      B. Generalization 21
      C. Inline methods 23
      D. Inline classes 23
   2.5. Automated build and continuous integration 24
   2.6. Collective code ownership 24
   2.7. Case Study 24
   2.8. Brief Introduction 25
   2.9. What are the reasons to take an Agile Certification 26
   2.9.1. What is PMI-ACP® certification 28
   2.9.2. Benefits of PMI-ACP® certification 28
   2.9.3. What is SAFe® Agilist 28
   2.9.4. Benefits of SAFe® Agilist 28
   2.9.5. PMI-ACP® vs. SAFe® Agilist : Key Differentiators 29
   2.9.6. How to judge the Agile Certification which is a best fit for your career 32
   2.9.7. Conclusion 32
   3.0. Top 100 Plus Scrum Master Interview Questions and Answers 33
   3.1. So, what is Scrum? 33
   3.2. Why would I need a Scrum Master certification? 33
   3.3. SCRUM Nuts and Bolts 34
   3.4. Who is a Scrum Master? 34

3.5. WHAT IS A "USER STORY" IN SCRUM?	34
3.6. WHAT ARE THE THREE MAIN ARTIFACTS OF THE SCRUM PROCESS?	35
3.7. WHAT DO YOU UNDERSTAND BY THE TERM SCRUM SPRINT? WHAT IS ITS DURATION?	35
3.8. DESCRIBE THE ROLE OF A PRODUCT OWNER.	35
3.9. HOW DOES THE SCRUM MASTER HELP THE PRODUCT OWNER?	35
4.0. HOW DOES THE SCRUM MASTER SERVE THE ORGANIZATION?	36
4.1. WHY IS AGILE METHODOLOGY NECESSARY?	36
4.2. EXPLAIN SCRUM OVERVIEW	36
4.3. WHAT ARE THE FIVE PHASES OF RISK MANAGEMENT?	38
4.4. WHAT ARE THE MAIN TOOLS USED IN A SCRUM PROJECT?	38
4.5. HOW CAN A SCRUM MASTER TRACK THE PROGRESS OF A SPRINT?	38
THIS GRAPH SHOWS, EACH DAY, A NEW ESTIMATE OF HOW MUCH WORK REMAINS UNTIL THE TEAM IS FINISHED.	38
4.6. WHAT IS TIMEBOXING IN SCRUM?	40
4.7. IS CANCELLING A SPRINT POSSIBLE? WHO CAN CANCEL A SPRINT?	40
4.8. HOW IS ESTIMATION IN A SCRUM PROJECT DONE? WHAT ARE THE TECHNIQUES USED FOR ESTIMATION?	40
4.9. WHAT ARE THE ROLES INVOLVED IN THE SCRUM FRAMEWORK?	40
5.0. WHAT IS THE DIFFERENCE BETWEEN CHANGE MANAGEMENT IN A WATERFALL AND IN AN AGILE SCRUM?	40
5.1. WHAT IS THE PURPOSE OF A DAILY SCRUM?	40
5.2. WHAT DO YOU UNDERSTAND BY THE TERM SCOPE CREEP? HOW DO YOU PREVENT IT FROM HAPPENING?	43
5.3. WHAT ARE THE MOST COMMON RISKS IN A SCRUM PROJECT?	43
5.4. WHAT DO YOU UNDERSTAND BY MINIMUM VIABLE PRODUCT IN SCRUM?	43
5.5. WHAT IS THE MAJOR ADVANTAGE OF USING SCRUM?	43
5.6. WHAT DOES DOD MEAN? HOW CAN THIS BE ACHIEVED?	43
5.7. WHAT IS VELOCITY IN SCRUM?	45
5.8. LIST OUT THE DISADVANTAGES OF SCRUM	45
5.9. SCRUM PHASES AND PROCESSES	46
6.0. SCRUM FLOW	46
6.1. DEFINITION OF READY	46
6.2. PDCA CYCLE IN SCRUM	47
6.3. WHY SCRUM MASTER IS A SERVANT LEADER?	47
6.4. WHAT FACTOR DECIDES YOU WHETHER YOU WILL DO PROJECT IN SCRUM WAY?	48
6.5. SCRUM REAL LIFE ISSUE	48
6.6. WHAT DID YOU DO AS SCRUM MASTER TO PREVENT SCOPE CREEP?	48
6.7. EXAMPLE OF ONE POSITIVE RISK IN YOUR SCRUM PROJECT	48
6.8. EXAMPLE OF ONE NEGATIVE RISK IN YOUR SCRUM PROJECT	49
6.9. WHAT ARE THE MAIN REASONS FOR CRASHING SCHEDULE IN YOUR SCRUM PROJECT?	49
7.0. CAN WE USE DEVOPS IN YOUR SAP SCRUM PROJECT?	49
7.1. IN SCRUM, WHERE CUSTOMERS ARE INVOLVED?	49

- 7.2. What makes daily SCRUM a waste of time? 49
- 7.3. What techniques are used in daily SCRUM? 49
- 7.4. Who attends daily SCRUM? 50
- 7.5. What are the differences between Product backlog and Sprint backlog? 50
- 7.6. MoSCoW Prioritization technique 50
- 7.7. Scrum master certification exam sample questions 51
- 7.8. Important tips to prepare for an interview 51
- 7.9. Conclusion 51
- 8.0. Common Agile Product Development Myths 52
- 9.0. Three Types of "Scrum Teams" 54
- 10.0. Agile Budget Management 55
- 11.0. Agile Contract Management 57
- 12.0. Agile – Key Takeaways 59
- History of Agile 61
- WHAT IS AGILE? 62
- WHY CHOOSE AGILE? 62
- Benefits of Agile process 63
- Everything is not good 63
- SUMMARY 63
- 13. Quiz Session 64
- 14.0. Agile – Maturity assessment 66

Chapter 2 - DevOps Introduction 87
- 2.1. Principles of DevOps 89
- 2.2. Key Components of DevOps 90
- 2.3. DevOps Capabilities 91
- 2.4. DevOps Purpose & Objectives 92
- 2.5. DevOps Triggering Points 92
- 2.6. DevOps and People, Process and Technology 93
- 2.7. DevOps "Why" & "What" 94
- 2.8. DevOps – Key Takeaways 95
- 2.9. DevOps – Impediments 96
- 3.0. DevOps – Value Stream Example 97
- 3.1. DevOps Framework – Definitions and Overview 98
- Why DevOps 98
- 3.2. DevOps follows CALMS model 99
- 3.3. DevOps – Work Practices vs Phase 99
- 3.4. DevOps – Work Products 100
- 3.5. DevOps Practice - Continuous Business Planning 100
- 3.6. DevOps Practice - Collaborative Development 101
- 3.7. DevOps Practice - Continuous Testing 102
- 3.8. DevOps Practice - Continuous Deployments 102

3.9. DevOps Practice - Continuous Monitoring 103
4.0. DevOps Practice - Continuous Customer Feedback and Optimization 104
5.0. DevOps Capabilities – Framework Model & Principles 105
5.1. DevOps "Capability Framework Model" 105
5.2. DevOps "Capability Framework Principles" 106
5.3 DevOps "Operating Model" Framework 107
5.4 DevOps "Tools" with "SDLC Phases" - Demo 108
5.5 DevOps "Tooling Framework" – VALUE Chain DEMO 108
5.6 SDLC / ALM Framework- Phase & Tool Example - DEMO 108
5.7 DevOps "Continuous Business Planning" 109
5.8 DevOps "Continuous Integration & Continuous Testing" 110
5.9 DevOps "Continuous Deployment & Release Management" 110
5.10 DevOps "Continuous Release Management" 111
5.11 DevOps "Continuous Release & Deployment Automation" 112
5.12 DevOps "Capabilities" using "Quality Assurance" 113
5.13 DevOps "Continuous Delivery" with in-built "Quality Assurance" 114
5.14 DevOps "Capabilities" with in-built "Quality Assurance" 115
5.15. DevOps for Testing – Within SDLC Framework 116
5.15.1 SDLC (Testing Phase): Testing Framework for Agile Projects, using
  DevOps Methods 116
5.16. DevOps "Path to Production Model" 118
5.17. Process Comparisons – Traditional versus DevOps 119
5.18.1. Change Management Process Comparisons – Traditional versus DevOps 120
5.18.2. Quality Management Process Comparisons – Traditional vs DevOps 122
5.19. Agile vs DevOps 124
6. DevOps Implementation – Approach and Guidelines 126
6.1. DevOps "Design Guiding Principles" 126
6.2. DevOps "Implementation Approach" 127
6.3. DevOps "Implementation Considerations" 127
6.4. DevOps Modelling "per Product Types" 128
6.5. DevOps "Capability Modelling per XaaS Types Components" 130
6.6. DevOps "Tools Modelling Solution" 130
6.7. DevOps Capabilities Model within "SDLC Framework" 132
7. DevOps – Case Study 1 133
8. DevOps – Case Study 2 137
9. Appendix – Backup / References 138
10. Glossary 139
11.0. DevOps – Key Takeaways 139
12.0. DevOps – Top 100 Plus DevOps Interview Questions and Answers 142
13.0 . DevOps all-Inclusive Self-Assessment Checklist featuring more than 100
  new and updated real-time business case-based questions 172
14.0 . GIT – Tips & Tricks 219

15.0 . TEST YOUR KNOWLEDGE 230

Introduction

For decades, technology and business leaders have struggled to balance agility, reliability, automation and security, and the consequences of failure are always significant. The effective management of technology is critical for business competitiveness. High-performing organizations are 2.5 times more likely to exceed profitability, market share, and productivity goals. The Agile & DevOps handbook shows leaders how to create the cultural norms and the technical best practices necessary to maximize organizational learning, increase employee satisfaction, win in the marketplace, enhance Customer / business delight and capture new business.

If you are a tech developer, IT Consultant, Agile Coach, Scrum Master, Product Owner, Leader, Manager, Sr. Manager, part of product management team or IT operator, then this book is perfect for you in order to increase profitability, exceed productivity goals and elevate work culture through Agile & DevOps methodology. So, if you want to know what the basic principles of Agile & DevOps movement are and how to incorporate Agile & DevOps concept and practices into your own organization. This book will guide you through the world of the Agile & DevOps and through its main principles so you can greatly increase organizational potential and reduce the risk of failure. Learn why all major organizations are adopting the Agile & DevOps methodology and follow their success story with Agile & DevOps.

John Willis says - If you can't measure you can't improve. A successful DevOps implementation will measure everything it can as often as it can… performance metrics, process metrics and even people metrics.

The book has been written in such a way that the concepts are explained in detail, giving adequate emphasis on real-life examples. All the tools you need to an in-depth DevOps Self-Assessment Maturity model. Featuring 100 PLUS new and updated case-based questions, organized into seven core areas of process design, this Self-Assessment will help you identify areas in which DevOps improvements can be made.

To make clarity of the programming examples, logic is explained properly as well discussed using comments in program itself. The real-time examples are discussed in detail from simple to complex taking into consideration the requirement of IT consultants. Various sample projects are included in the book and are written in simple language so as to give IT consultants the basic idea of developing projects in Agile & DevOps. The examples given in book are user-focused and have been highly updated including topics, figures, strategies, best practices and real-life examples, demos and case studies.

You will explore DevOps process maturity frameworks and progression models with checklist templates for each phase of DevOps. This self-assessment empowers people to do just that - whether their title is entrepreneur, coach, leader, manager, consultant, (Vice-) President, CEO, CTO, COO, CIO etc... - they are the people who rule the future. They are the people who ask the right questions to make DevOps investments work better.

This DevOps all-inclusive self-assessment enables you to be that person.

The book features more on practical approach with more examples covering topics from simple to complex one, addressing many of the core concepts and advance topics also.

The book is divided into the following sections:
- 600 PLUS Real-time Agile & DevOps interview questions and answers
- Numerous Tricky Real-time Agile & DevOps Case Studies and Demos
- DevOps all-Inclusive Self-Assessment Checklist for Maturity Model featuring 400 PLUS new and updated case-based questions
- The state of agility
- Different Agile frameworks (extreme programming, SCRUM, Kanban, crystal methodologies, SAFe, dynamic software development methods, feature driven development, lean software development)
- Common Agile Product Development & Test Automation Myths
- Dictionary of Tools & techniques of Agile and DevOps
- Different Types of Agile Certifications - Tips & Tricks
- Estimation techniques used in Agile and DevOps
- DevOps, Lean, ITSM, Agile value stream examples
- DevOps Implementation – Approach & Guidelines
- Change Management Process - DevOps
- Quality Management Process - DevOps
- Get to know what are continuous integration, continuous delivery, and continuous deployment
- DevOps - Continuous Business Planning
- DevOps - Continuous Integration & Continuous Testing
- DevOps - Continuous Deployment & Release Management
- DevOps - Continuous Release & Deployment Automation
- DevOps - Continuous Testing
- DevOps - Continuous Monitoring
- DevOps - Continuous Customer Feedback And Optimization
- DevOps - DevOps "Continuous Delivery" With In-Built "Quality Assurance"
- Continuous Improvement – Agile and DevOps
- Agile & DevOps main goal and challenges
- Integrate recent advances in DevOps and process design strategies into practice according to best practice guidelines
- Diagnose Agile & DevOps projects, initiatives, organizations, businesses and processes using accepted diagnostic standards and practices
- Technical best practices
- Service Oriented Architecture, Client Server Architecture, 4+1 Architecture View Model
- **Infrastructure as a Service (IaaS), Platform as a Service (PaaS), Software as a Service (SaaS)**
- Agile Budget Management
- Agile Contract Management
- Software development and Agile

Chapter 1 - Agile Introduction

Agile began as an iterative, collaborative, value-driven approach to developing software.
It was originally conceived as a framework to help structure work on complex projects with dynamic, unpredictable characteristics.
But since then, it has evolved into somewhat of a philosophy or world view, with a set of well-articulated values and principles common between Agile's many varieties.

1.1. Agile manifesto and key agile principles

1.1.1. Agile manifesto

Agile Manifesto

We are uncovering better ways of developing software by doing it and helping others do it.
Through this work we have come to value:

Individuals and interactions over processes and tools
Working software over comprehensive documentation
Customer collaboration over contract negotiation
Responding to change over following a plan

While there is value in the items on the right, we value the items on the left more.

Figure 1.0 : Agile Manifesto
Image Source: AgileAlliance.org

1.1.2. Agile principles

- Highest priority is customer satisfaction, achieved by the early and continuous delivery of valuable software
- Welcome the changing requirements, even those that arise late in development
- Continuous focus on delivering shippable customer priority deliverables in an iterative and incremental way
- Working software is frequently delivered, from a couple of weeks or months, preference to the shorter timescale
- Throughout the project, the business people and developers must work together
- Projects are built around motivated individuals - support and trust them to get the job done
- Face-to-face conversation is the most efficient and effective method of conveying information
- The working software is the principal measure of progress
- Agile processes promote sustainable development, the ability to maintain a constant pace
- Good design and continuous attention to technical excellence enhances agility
- Simplicity and continuous focus on % of work done rather than % of effort spent by team
- Requirements, best architecture, and design emerge from all self-organising teams
- Frequently reflect, how to improve efficiency

1.1.3. Key agile principles

- Focus on the customer and business value
- Iterative and fast development
- Flexible, adaptive, and continuously improving
- Collaboration and team work
- Empowered and self-directed teams

1.2. Agile Values

Trust: Among the various stake holders (team, Scrum Master, Product owner, Project manager) plays a vital role in making Agile successful.

Respect: Individuals have to respect and consider the opinion of all the stake holders, no matter even if a team member is a fresher to the team.

Openness: Team/Scrum Master should be open to the management and the product owner while providing the status updates, highlighting risks (both internal and external risks).

Courage: Team should have the courage to say *NO* to the management if we cannot commit to the delivery with appropriate reasons.

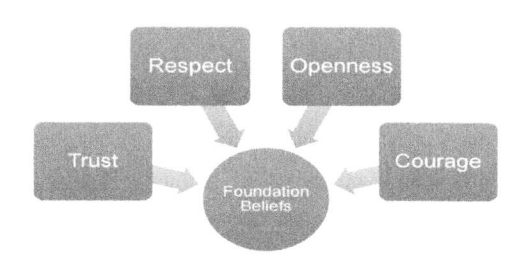

Figure 1.1 : Agile values

1.3. Traditional life cycle versus Agile development

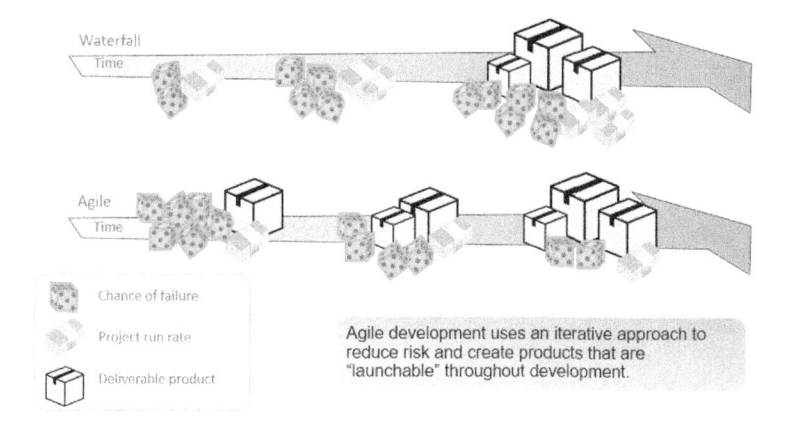

Figure 1.2 : Waterfall vs. Agile

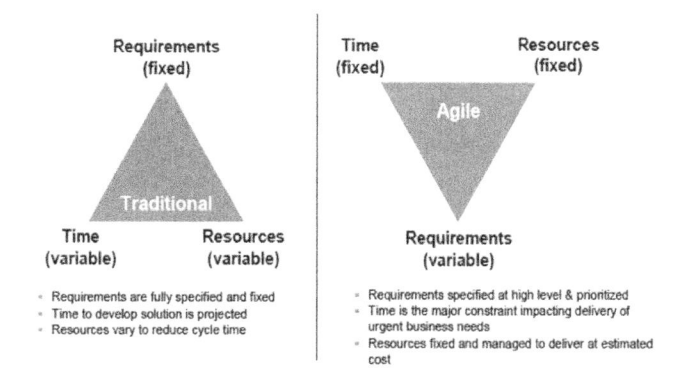

Figure 1.3 : Waterfall vs. Agile – Triple constraints

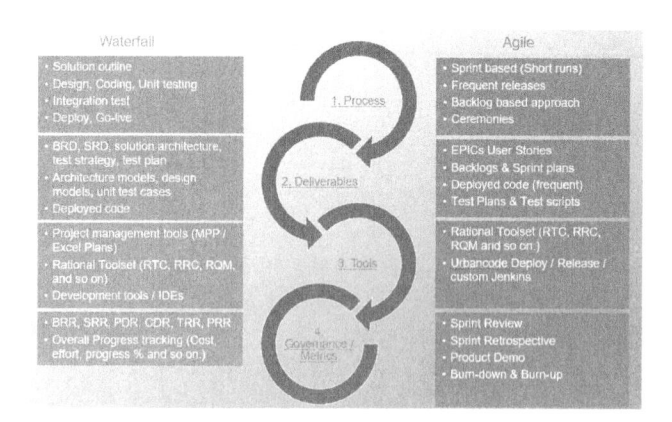

Figure 1.4 : Waterfall vs. Agile – High level comparison

1.4. AGILITY VERSUS AGILE

Agility

It is the property of an organization to sense and respond to market changes and continuously deliver value to customers.

Agile

An organizational approach and mindset defined by the values and principles of the Agile Manifesto, often practiced through a framework like Scrum.

1.5. The State of Agility

A vast majority of organizations recognize the importance of agility and its rewards. Yet agility can be elusive: Many are struggling to translate this nearly 20-year-old software development strategy into a broader management concept. To successfully transform, today's organizations need to embrace agility from strategy to execution, and enterprise-wide.

The time to do so is now. Our survey findings indicate that two-thirds (66%) of organizations have experienced less than 10% growth in revenue over the most recent fiscal year. Trends like this make the ability to react quickly to emerging trends, design better products, enhance team morale, and meet sky-high customer expectations more critical than ever.

Figure 1. The top benefits of organizational agility

Faster time to market — 60%
Faster innovation — 59%
Improved non-financial results — 58%
Improved employee morale — 57%
Ability to attract/hire top talent — 57%
Improved competitiveness — 56%
Improved financial results — 55%
Ability to better manage across geographies/verticals — 55%

Figure 1.5 : The top benefits of organizational agility
Image Source: Forbesinsights

Organizations already recognize the value of agility to the enterprise. A staggering 81% of all survey respondents consider it to be the most important characteristic of a successful organization. And 82% of respondents consider agility to be very or extremely important to an organization's success and competitiveness. Among the most popular Agile approaches selected by respondents: Scrum, cited by more than three-quarters (77%) of leaders.

Figure 2. Functions in which organizations are most Agile

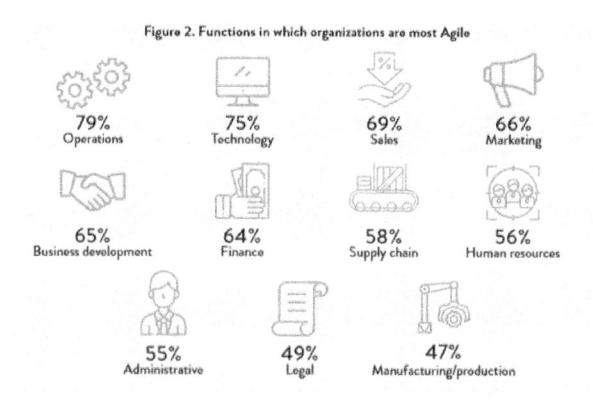

- 79% Operations
- 75% Technology
- 69% Sales
- 66% Marketing
- 65% Business development
- 64% Finance
- 58% Supply chain
- 56% Human resources
- 55% Administrative
- 49% Legal
- 47% Manufacturing/production

Figure 1.6 : Functions in which organizations are most Agile
Image Source: Forbesinsights

"Agility is a prerequisite to stay competitive in the long run; it is not optional," says Joerg Erlemeier, chief operating officer of Nokia, a Finnish multinational telecommunications and consumer electronics company. "Being Agile enables us to respond faster and better meet our customers' requests." Agile initiatives at Nokia include redesigning business processes, creating a customer-centric supply chain and introducing smaller, more nimble teams.

There's good reason for the popularity of organizational agility. For those that succeed at achieving greater agility, leaders and laggards see many benefits, including faster time to market, faster innovation and improved non-financial results, to name just a few.

Toyota Motor Corporation is just one company reaping the benefits of increased agility. By working "in small batches" and creating continuous process flows like the Toyota Production System, Nigel Thurlow, chief of Agile for Toyota Connected (the global technology strategy business unit for Toyota), says the company's Kentucky manufacturing plant can upgrade systems that support the plant machinery in six days—a fraction of the seven weeks once required for the exact same task. "When you're working in short sprints and small batches, you're able to see the value delivered more rapidly," he says. "But more importantly, you're able to catch your mistakes more rapidly, change your mind and make decisions based upon emerging requirements."

Such flexibility is imperative in today's business environment, as the rapid pace of technology, innovation and development requires organizations to deliver results faster than ever. But agility is about more than getting products out the door faster than your competitors. Agile began as a response to the failings of traditional software development. Faced with blown budgets and missed deadlines, organizations turned to Agile to increase the rate at which they could create new products and roll out updates.

Figure 3. Types of approaches currently employed by leaders and laggards

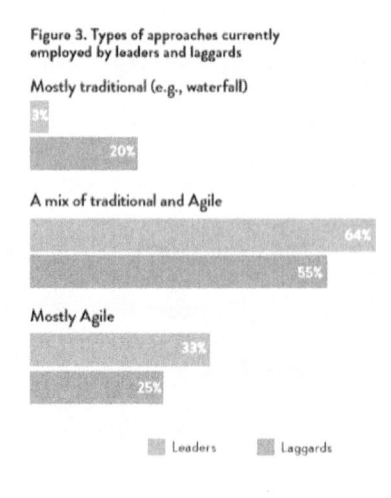

Mostly traditional (e.g., waterfall)
- Leaders: 3%
- Laggards: 20%

A mix of traditional and Agile
- Leaders: 64%
- Laggards: 55%

Mostly Agile
- Leaders: 33%
- Laggards: 25%

Figure 1.7 : Types of approaches currently employed by leaders and laggards
Image Source: Forbesinsights

1.6. Three Steps to increase Agility

1. Create a C-suite with an Agile mindset.
2. Hire and develop the right mix of talent.
3. Foster an Agile-friendly culture and organizational structure.

These strategies enable organizations, many of which are being upended by innovation, to expand agility throughout the organization for sustainable business growth and transformation success.

Solving a client's issue may require many complex work streams, so we set up a sprint...It's a way of getting people to be collaborative, take accountability and feel empowered.

-- TAMARA INGRAM CHIEF EXECUTIVE OFFICER, J. WALTER THOMPSON COMPANY

1.7. Agile Framework

Extreme Programming (XP)	SCRUM	Unified Process	Crystal	Scaled Agile Framework	Dynamic Systems Development Method (DSDM)	Feature Driven Dev	Kanban
-Based on values of simplicity, communication, feedback, courage, and respect -Start with simple solution, add complexity through refactoring	-Small teams of 5-9 people -"Backlog" defined requirements that will be addressed in each Sprint -Daily 15 min. Scrum meeting to discuss work for the day	-Simplified version of Rational Unified Process – reduced	-Frequent Delivery -Reflective improvement	-interactive knowledge base for implementing agile practices at enterprise scale -Based on Lean and Agile principles	-3 primary phases: Pre-Project, Project Life-Cycle, Post-Project	-Develop feature list, Plan, Design, Build by Feature	-Incremental, Evolutionary Change -Kanban board help team understand how they are doing and also what to do next

Agile Techniques: The above methods involve a range of techniques including:

Test-driven development	Continuous integration	Static Analysis
Planning game	Design improvement	Coding standard
Pair Programming	Small releases	Sustainable pace
Refactoring	Simple design	Whole team

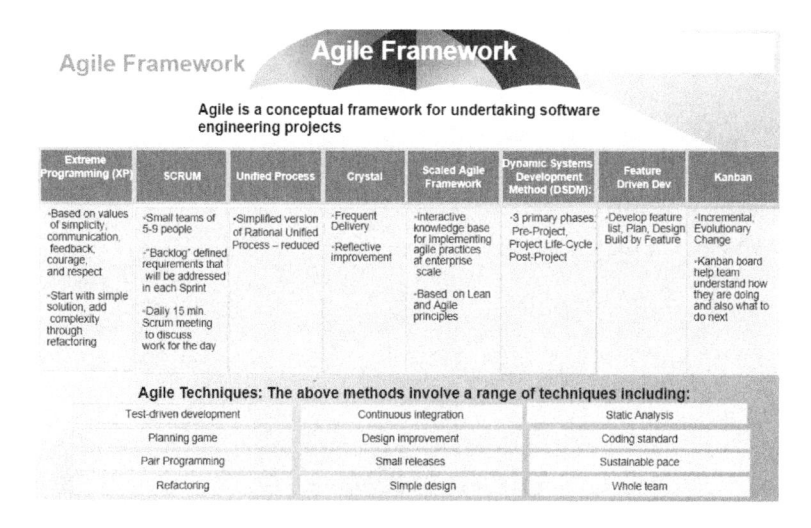

Figure 1.8 : Agile Framework

Agile methodology encourages the continuous iteration of advancement and testing during the project software development life cycle.
Following are some Agile frameworks that can be implemented within Agile projects:
1. Extreme programming
2. Crystal methodologies
3. Scrum
4. Lean software development
5. Feature driven development
6. Dynamic software development methods

Extreme programming is the successful method of developing Agile software. It focuses on customer satisfaction.
To develop the software, extreme programming requires maximum interaction with customers.
It divides the entire software development life cycle into short growth sequences.

1.8. Agile Concepts

The core ideas in Agile:

Adaptive: The process and the team must be flexible.

Iterative: Agile development introduces efficient products in stages, which are evolving sets of *completed and working software.*

People-oriented: The organisation should support teams and people as they are an essential element for the success of a project.

1.9. Benefits of Agile

- Speed to market
- Right product
- Quality
- Flexibility
- Transparency
- Risk management
- Cost control

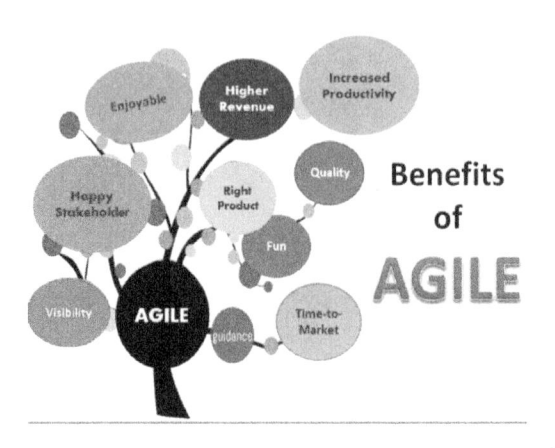

Figure 1.9 : Benefits of Agile
Image source: https://www.prepaway.com/

Agile training and certification helps practitioners to enhance their skill sets by interaction.

2.0. Technical best practices

The following are some technical best practices to be followed:
- Test-driven development
- Continuous refactoring
- Automated builds and continuous integration
- Collective code ownership
- Frequent design and code reviews
- Automated acceptance and regression tests

2.1. Test driven development

The flow chart describes the process followed for test-driven development.

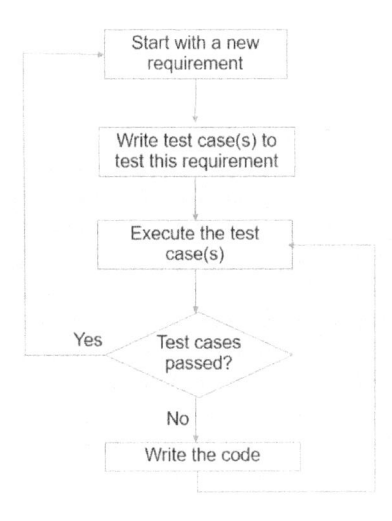

Figure 1.10 : Test driven development

2.2. Advantages of test driven development

The following are some advantages of test-driven development:
- Makes the developer **first think** about *how to use* the component and only then about *how to implement*
- There is no code without a TEST; thus ensures all requirements are tested
- Greater level of confidence in the code
- Wide test coverage eliminates defects in the early stage
- Increased code coverage

2.3. Tools of Test driven development

Specific tools are available to support test-driven development.
- Framework for automating the unit tests
    - Example: Junit, JMeter
- **Integrated development environment (IDE)**
- For writing tests, using auto-completion and generation of missing code
- For running the tests
- For refactoring
    - Example: Eclipse, **Rational Application Developer (RAD)**
- Build environment
- For executing tests automatically and during the build process
- For computing code coverage
- For generating test reports
    - Example: Maven, Jenkins.

2.4. Code refactoring

Code refactoring is the process of restructuring existing code without affecting its functionality.

Advantages
- Helps improve code quality, reusability and maintainability
- Helps improve performance of application

Techniques
- Increasing level of abstraction
- Generalization
- Inline methods
- Inline class

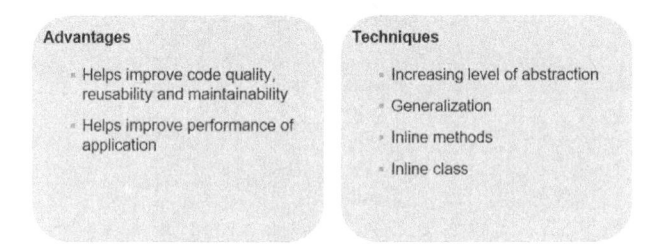

Figure 1.11 : Code refactoring technique

2.4.1 Techniques of Code refactoring

The following are the techniques of code refactoring:
- Increasing level of abstraction
- Generalization
- Inline methods
- Inline classes

    a. **Increasing level of abstraction**

- **Before (Pseudo Code)**

```java
public class NormalFieldClass {
  public String name;

  public static void main(String[] args)
  {
    NormalFieldClass example1 = new NormalFieldClass();
    example1.name = "myName";
    System.out.println("My name is " + example1.name);
  }
}
```

- **After (Pseudo Code)**

```java
public class EncapsulatedFieldClass {
  private String name;

  public String name()
    {
      return name;

    }

  public void setName(String newName)

    {
      name = newName;

    }

  public static void main(String[] args)
    {
      EncapsulatedFieldClass example1 = new EncapsulatedFieldClass();
      example1.setName ("myName");
      System.out.println ("My name is " + example1.getName());

    }

}
```

b. **Generalization**

Before (Pseudo code)

```java
public class TestOverriding {
  public static void main(String aga[]){
    Parrot bird=new Parrot();
    bird.fly();
  }
```

```java
}
class Bird{
   private  void eats(){
      System.out.println("......");
   }
}
class Parrot extends Bird{
   public void doStuff(){
      System.out.println("I am parrot , and I am doing stuff");
   }
   public void fly(){
      System.out.println("Bird is flying");
   }
}
class Pigeon extends Bird{
   public void doStuff(){
      System.out.println("I am Pigeon , and I am White");
   }
   public void fly(){
      System.out.println("Bird is flying");
   }
}
```

After (Pseudo code)

```java
public class TestOverriding {
   public static void main(String aga[]){
      Parrot bird=new Parrot();
      bird.fly();
   }
}
class Bird{
   private  void fly(){
      System.out.println("Bird is flying");
   }
    private  void eats(){
      System.out.println("......");
   }
}
class Parrot extends Bird{
   public void doStuff(){
      System.out.println("I am parrot , and I am doing stuff");
   }
}
class Pigeon extends Bird{
   public void doStuff(){
      System.out.println("I am Pigeon , and I am White");
   }
}
```

c. **Inline methods**

Before (Pseudo code)

```
int getRating() {
   return(moreThanFiveLateDeliveries()) ? 2 : 1;
}
boolean moreThanFiveLateDeliveries() {
   return (numberOfLateDeliveries > 5);
}
```

After (Pseudo code)

```
int getRating() {
   return ((numberOfLateDeliveries > 5) ? 2 : 1);
}
```

d. **Inline classes**

Before (Pseudo code)

```
class Person{
   private string PersonName;
   private string Address;
   public int getTelephoneNumber() { }
}
class telephoneNumber extends Person{
   private int areaCode;
   private int number;
   public int getTelephoneNumber() { }
}
```

After (Pseudo code)

```
class Person{
   private string PersonName;
   private string Address;
   private int areaCode;
   private int number;
   public int getTelephoneNumber() { }
}
```

2.5. Automated build and continuous integration

Continuous Integration (**CI**) is the practice of merging all developer working copies (code) with a shared mainstream several times a day. This includes the following:
- Developer checks-in the code as and when development is completed
- Building EAR/JAR scheduled as per desired frequency (**Build process automated**)
- Automated unit test cases (UT) / Regression test cases executed after every build
- Build failure / Issues with test cases report updated to developers

2.5.1. Tools supporting CI
Build Server (Example: Maven, Jenkins) are used:
- As code repository
- For automating builds
- To trigger UT execution
- To generate reports

2.5.2. Advantage of CI
CI helps to identify integration issues at an early stage and hence reduces re-work effort.

2.6. Collective code ownership

Ownership:

- Everyone is responsible for all the code. Therefore, everyone is allowed to change any part of the code.
- Pair programming contributes to this practice. It helps create code visibility to more developers.

Pros
- Speeds up the development process since multiple programmers can fix the issue
- Eliminates dependency on owner of the code

Cons
- Risk of errors being introduced by the programmers who cannot foresee dependencies – well defined unit test cases should address this problem

2.7. Case Study

A developer's typical day

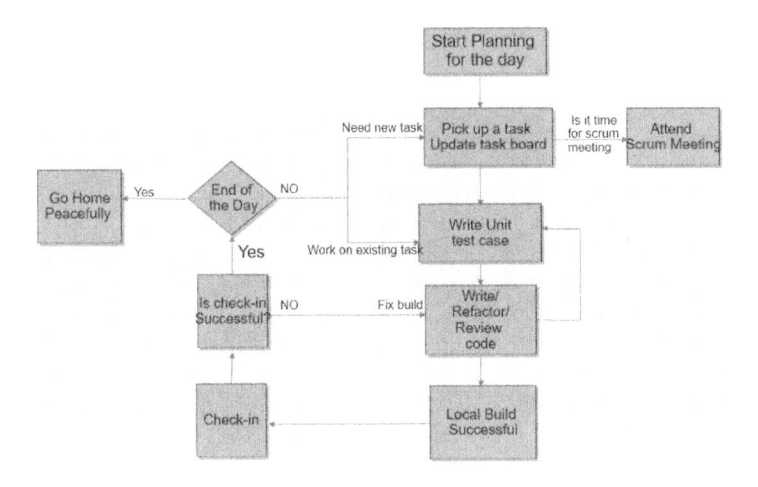

Figure 1.12 : A developer's typical day

A tester's typical day

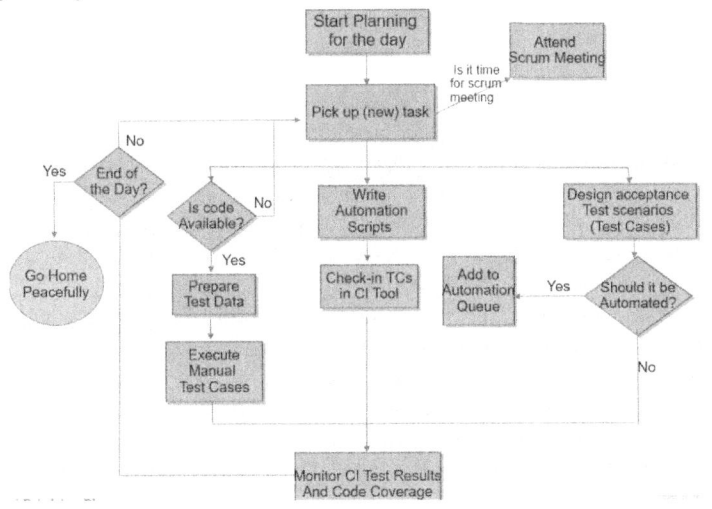

Figure 1.13 : A tester's typical day

2.8. Brief Introduction

Agile is going to create 21st Century's business model disruptions. So, it is important to choose the right agile certifications for your career growth. This adds some confusion to the young professionals. They have stepped into Agile world recently.
It applies to fresher too. They are planning to build their career in Agile project management. They remain concerned about, which role should they choose to make the career? In fact, they struggle to

understand, whether there is any difference in these roles or are they same? And if they are same, why are they are named different?

This article uncovers the differences between PMI-ACP® and SAFe® Agilist agile certifications. This is definitely a good article to read and understand the nuances of these roles. Who is a PMI Agile Certified Practitioner? What does a **SAFe Agilist (SA)** do?

I would start with the importance of these agile certifications need. This will lay the foundation for better clarity on the subject of discussion. Then, I will discuss the differences between these two agile certifications.

2.9. What are the reasons to take an Agile Certification

- Agile certified consultant can deliver project and product as per end user perspective.
- Agile certified consultant can deliver project and product in incremental & iterative way. He/she can adhere to extreme programming & lean principles (as applicable).
- Agile certified consultant can deliver project and product to maximize ROI. Agile certified consultant can maximize the stakeholders delight by gaining in-depth knowledge in Agile.
- Scrum / Agile certification is must to deliver work with best team velocity / productivity. Agile certified consultant can maintain good first time right products quality. Here, the teams are self-organized, cross functional.

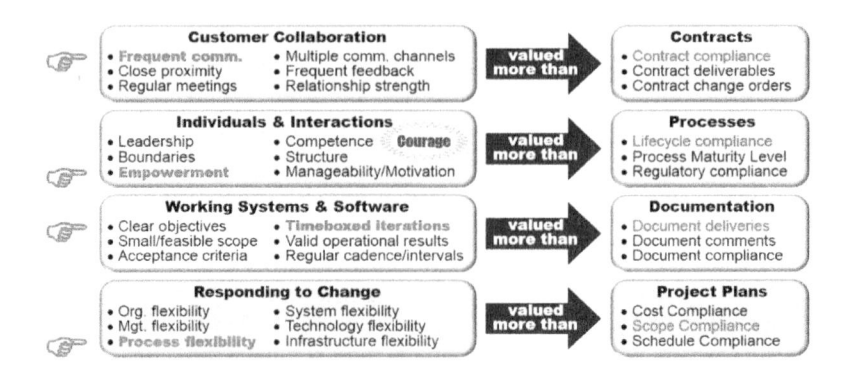

Figure 1.14 : Agile Manifesto illustration

- To get more salary and getting promotion Agile Certification is the must
- Agile certified consultant can get different tips & traps in Agile Project Management. You can get different delivery management strategies and tips on customer centric focus. It helps him / her to create transparency at workplace via different Scrum ceremonies.

- Agile Certification helps consultant to stay aligned with current industry trends. Agile Certification helps consultant to adhere to best practices.
- After agile certification you can become Agile community member. Thus, you can enhance your skill sets by iteration with your peers. You can inspect, adapt through transparent continuous feedback loops.
- Agile certified consultant can act as a change agent. He/she can drive organizational change.
- Agile certification helps consultant to improve their skill sets in different techniques, servant leadership.
- Agile training and certification helps consultant for facilitating stakeholder discussion, road mapping. It also helps him / her for product discovery.
  It also helps him/her improving and managing the product backlog, product management. Agile certified consultant can also perform effective release planning.
  Agile certified consultant can do effective implementation of engineering practices, technical debt.
- Sometimes volume of work is unpredictable. Often bottleneck situation arises. Then it is very tough for the consultant to handle it.
  But Agile certified consultant can manage the flow of work. He / she can do mapping between customer demand and supply.
- Agile certified consultant can manage project and product with good quality. Agile certified consultant can deliver projects as per signed SLA or KPIs. He/she can deliver products through incremental & iterative shippable products delivery. He/she can abide by Agile / scrum and Lean values, principles, and worldview.
  It helps him/her to focus on quick response to the proposed changes. It comprises short duration iterations.
- Agile training and certification helps consultant in scaling Organizational development, Conflict resolution. It also helps consultant in Agile facilitation and coaching.
- Agile certified consultant can find creative ways to help organizations. He/she can help his/her peers to adopt the Agile framework and capitalize on its benefits.

Be the change YOU want to see...

Roll up your sleeves and show them how it's done.

- Mahatma Gandhi

Choosing a certification that is best for you doesn't lead to the success that you deserve. The effectiveness of the course depends on the training provider.
So, always choose for Agile certification based on your experience.

2.9.1. What is PMI-ACP® certification

Project Management Institute (PMI) offers **Agile Certified Practitioner (ACP)** certification. It is for professionals currently using agile or are moving to agile practices.

Team leads, project leads or for leadership professionals can attend this certification.
It is also for *Being Agile* practitioners following daily agile principles and methodologies.

2.9.2. Benefits of PMI-ACP® certification

   a. Agile Certified Practitioner can apply Agile principles and values in different Agile methodologies. Like SCRUM, XP, Lean, KANBAN, and so on. So, it gives them better visibility.
   b. Better salary as the salary of a certified PMI ACP professional is about 28% higher than that a non-certified professional.
   c. Agile Certified Practitioner can perform as Change agent in continuous improvement initiatives. Thus, they can add values in their organization. So, it increases their credibility.
   d. Keeping up to current market trends.
   e. To manage the projects in an effective way as *Being Agile*.
   f. If your organization is looking forward to introduce Agile framework for achieving high end project goals, then PMI ACP certification is best to choose.
   g. Agile Certified Practitioner can do Agile risk management
   h. Agile Certified Practitioner can do Agile value stream analysis, value based prioritization
   i. Agile Certified Practitioner can do RCA using different statistical methods like five WHYs, fishbone diagram analysis.
   j. Agile Certified Practitioner can plan and manage Agile KPIs.
   k. Agile Certified Practitioner can plan and manage Agile Metrics.
   l. Agile Certified Practitioner can follow and drive Agile Manifesto, principles, values, tools, techniques in projects.

2.9.3. What is SAFe® Agilist

A Certified SAFe® Agilist practitioner is a lean agile change agent in large IT organization while working with multiple teams.

2.9.4. Benefits of SAFe® Agilist

   a. Better visibility, as a Certified SAFe® Agilist practitioner can apply Lean-Agile Mindset and principles.
   b. Better salary, as the salary of a certified SAFe Agilist professional is about 30% higher than that a non-certified professional.
   c. Certified SAFe® Agilist practitioner can drive many value added activities in an organization. So, it increases their credibility.
   d. Keeping up to current market trends.

e. A Certified SAFe® Agilist practitioner can manage portfolios of agile teams and can do lean agile budgeting.
   f. A Certified SAFe® Agilist practitioner can plan and execute program increments.

SAFe Agilist and Scaled Agilist terms are synonyms. This is the position given to a person who has completed the course Leading SAFe. The two-day informational course and certification exam which creates the following outcomes:
- Successful application in Agile enterprise environments.
- Recognition of Lean-Agile mindset.
- Development and empowerment of consultants through Lean portfolio.
- Support of Agile leadership principles. It drives itself to organizational transformation.
- Continuous iterative incremental cycle of continuous improvement. You can use dot voting technique for this.

2.9.5. PMI-ACP® vs. SAFe® Agilist : Key Differentiators

Sr. No.	Description	PMI-ACP®	SAFe® Agilist
1	Training	It requires 21 Professional development units PMI ACP training. It can be classroom or online training from **Registered Education Provider (R.E.P.)**	It is mandatory to attend two days SAFe agile certification classroom training. The course covers SAFe defined content by training providers.
2	Certification Course Fee	- PMI ACP certification cost for online self learning is $400. - PMI ACP certification cost for live online training is Rs. 34930. Visit the site to have detailed info about PMI ACP certification course. **PMI ACP certification provider URL –** https://www.greycampus.com/pmi-acp-training-	Various worldwide vendors provide the SAFe agile training and it costs around $1,000. Visit the site to have detailed info about SAFe agile certification course. **SAFe Agilist certification provider URL –** https://www.scaledagile.com/certification/which-course-is-right-for-me/

		instructor-led	
3	**Experience /Eligibility/ Prerequisites**	a. 2000 hours or 12 months of real-time project experience (earned in last five years) in managing project teams. b. Additionally, 1500 hours or 8 months of real-time Agile project experience (earned in last three years) with agile methodologies. c. 21 hours of Agile training in agile methodologies, values, lean agile principles, practices, tools and techniques. d. Secondary degree (associate's degree or high school diploma or global equal).	a. Five plus years' experience in business analysis, testing, software development, project or product management. b. Experience in SAFe SCRUM. He / She ensures scrum team's adherence to *Scrum* during agile projects.
4	**Exam Cost**	For PMI member agile certified practitioner PMI ACP certification cost is $435.00 (Computer based exam fee). For Non PMI member agile certified practitioner PMI ACP certification cost is $495.00 (Computer based exam fee). And, Paper based exam fee is: - $385 for PMI member, - $445 for Non PMI member.	Safe agile certification cost is $995 per course. Here first exam attempt is free.
5	**Course Content**	Agile project management training	SAFe certification training course table of contents includes the following:

		course table of contents include the following: - Many Agile methodologies like SCRUM, XP, Kanban, Lean. - Agile Manifesto, principles, values, tools, techniques - Scrum artefacts, roles, ceremonies, - Estimation techniques, Agile planning, monitoring and adapting, - Agile risk management, - Agile Metrics, - Agile value stream analysis, value based prioritization, - Agile product quality, - Communication, - Interpersonal skills. - Process improvements, Kaizen - Statistical methods like five WHYs, fishbone diagram analysis - Agile Contracting - Agile Project chartering - Agile hybrid models - Managing with Agile KPIs. **Agile Project Management certification exam** - 120 objective type questions to answer in three hours duration.	- Apply Lean-Agile Mindset and principles. - Plan and execute Program Increments. - Execute and release value through Agile Release Trains. - Build an Agile portfolio with Lean-Agile budgeting. - Apply DevOps principles - Apply SAFe principles for Product owner - Apply SAFe principles for Scrum master **SAFe agile certification exam** - 45 objective type questions to answer in 90 minutes duration - Passing score is 34 out of 45, i.e., 75% is the SAFe certification passing score.
6	**Certification Validity & Renewal**	- Earn 30 **Professional development units (PDUs)** in every 3 years. - Renewal of PMI ACP certification needs to be done in every 3 years.	You need to renew SAFe Agilist certification or scaled agile certification every year by paying renewal fee $100.

			- Renewal fee is $60.	
7	**Course Accreditation**	**Project Management Institute (PMI)** offers it.		Scaled Agile offers it.
8	**Salary**	The salary of a certified PMI ACP professional is about 28% higher than that a non-certified professional.		The salary of a certified SAFe Agilist professional is about 30% higher than that a non-certified professional.

2.9.6. How to judge the Agile Certification which is a best fit for your career

- It's 3 steps approach.
- Choose the Agile Certification which is best fit for purpose of your career path and as per your current job role & skill sets.
- We can correlate it in the below three step approach to choose the best Agile certification as per your current career path.

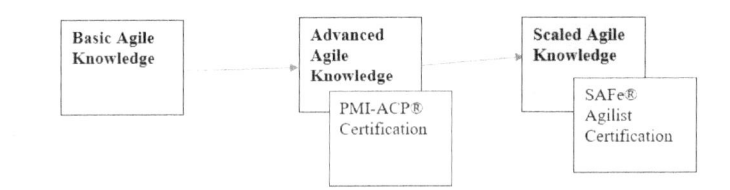

```
┌─────────────┐      ┌─────────────┐      ┌─────────────┐
│ Basic Agile │ ───▶ │  Advanced   │ ───▶ │ Scaled Agile│
│ Knowledge   │      │   Agile     │      │ Knowledge   │
└─────────────┘      │ Knowledge   │      │   SAFe®     │
                     │  PMI-ACP®   │      │  Agilist    │
                     │Certification│      │Certification│
                     └─────────────┘      └─────────────┘
```

Figure 1.15 : How to choose your Agile certification

2.9.7. Conclusion

Team leads, project leads or for leadership professionals can attend this certification.
It is also for *Being Agile* practitioners following daily agile principles and methodologies.
PMI-ACP certified consultant helps your company for achieving high end project goals.

PMI-ACP® Exam is not limited to Scrum Framework. It also includes other frameworks like Lean, Kanban, and XP. PMI-ACP® is strong examination compared to the basic Scrum Master certifications. You also need to take a classroom or online training before appearing in the exam.

SAFe Agilist could be an ideal choice for you if you are working with many teams in the adoption of Scaled Agile Framework in your enterprise.
SAFe Agilist and Scaled Agilist terms are synonyms. This is the position given to a person who has completed the course Leading SAFe.

Finally, it's imperative that a PMI Agile Certified Practitioner's role is more of a Leadership role. While SAFe Agilist's duties include more of facilitating and coaching role, the choice is yours, which certification to choose. It is in line with the capability you would like to grow in your professional life.

Choosing a certification that is best for you doesn't lead to the success you deserve. The effectiveness of course depends on best training provider. So, always choose based on your experience.

3.0. Top 100 Plus Scrum Master Interview Questions and Answers

Certified Scrum Masters are on high demand. Organizations seeking to adopt a more agile method now choose Scrum as their framework. Thus, a large part of the team's success depends on a skilled Scrum Master. It is on their hands to make a difference in the dynamics and performance of an agile team. Whether you are new to Scrum or already an expert, it is always beneficial to know how to prepare for a job interview in this field.

This article uncovers the different areas under which questions are asked and what are the most commonly asked ones. We hope that these will help you while preparing for your Scrum Master interview.

First, to shed some light on the subject of discussion, let's begin explaining the importance of Scrum certifications. We will then discuss a few tricky Scrum Master interview questions and best answers.

3.1. So, what is Scrum?

Scrum is a methodology based on agile principles, with the goal of allowing a team to organize better and be ready to change quickly. It emphasizes teamwork, communication, and speed across complex projects. The Scrum Master is the one who manages the process of how information is exchanged.

3.2. Why would I need a Scrum Master certification?

A Scrum Master certification demonstrates the core knowledge of the Scrum process. It is an added advantage as it proves the holder as a continuous learner. It shows ambition, which boosts professional growth. These are a few benefits of getting a Scrum certification:

- It provides with Scrum principles and skills.

- It prevents challenges and obstacles which may occur while using an Agile platform.

- It enhances team collaboration.

- It brings a change of mindset for the whole team.

With the growing demand for Scrum Masters, holding a certification adds a competitive advantage and builds a stronger professional credibility.

3.3. SCRUM Nuts and Bolts

Here are a few frequently asked questions that will help you prepare for your job interview:

3.4. Who is a Scrum Master?

The Scrum Master is responsible for supporting and promoting the Scrum. They assist their team in meeting their goals. They help managing project risks and mentor the team as its coach. The Scrum Master is also known as a servant leader, as they provide collaboration and motivate the team to deliver their best.

3.5. What is a "user story" in Scrum?

A user story is a tool used in Agile software development that captures the description of a feature from an end-user perspective. It describes, among others, the type of user and their motivations. A user story creates a simplified description of a user's requirements.

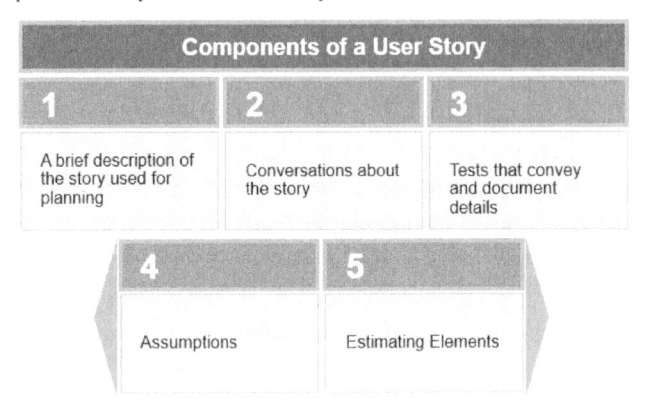

Components of a User Story

1. A brief description of the story used for planning
2. Conversations about the story
3. Tests that convey and document details
4. Assumptions
5. Estimating Elements

Figure 1.16 : Purpose of a user story

A User Story describes functionality that will be useful to a stakeholder of the system.

User Stories - Example

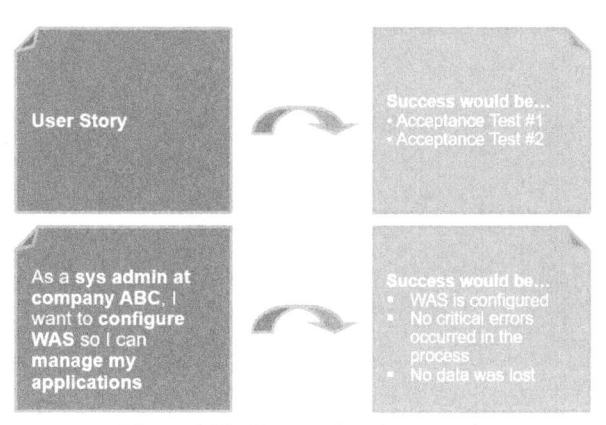

Figure 1.17 : User stories: An example

3.6. What are the three main artifacts of the Scrum process?

- Product Backlog
- Sprint Backlog
- Product Increment

3.7. What do you understand by the term Scrum Sprint? What is its duration?

A Scrum Sprint is a repeatable cycle during which the work is completed and made ready for review. The duration of the Scrum Sprint depends on the size of the project and the team working on it. Generally, it is under 30 days.

3.8. Describe the role of a Product Owner.

The Product Owner focuses on the success of the product, ensuring the business value of it. Their main responsibility is to identify and refine the Product Backlog items.

3.9. How does the Scrum Master help the Product Owner?

- Efficient Product Backlog management
- Helping the Scrum team in adopting a shared vision

- Understanding and practicing agility

- Facilitating Scrum events as requested or needed

4.0. How does the Scrum Master serve the organization?

- Helping in Scrum adoption.

- Acting as an Agile change agent.

- Helping the team, increasing productivity.

- Ensuring the iterative incremental cycle of continuous improvement. The *dot voting* technique is often used for this.

- Supporting Agile leadership principles, leading to organizational transformation.

4.1. Why is Agile methodology necessary?

- It helps achieving customer satisfaction with the rapid delivery of useful software.

- It eases potential changing requirements, even late in a company's development.

- Repeatedly delivers a working software, the main measurement of progress.

- It provides close, daily cooperation between the company and the developers.

- Having self-organizing teams brings as a result self-motivated team members.

- In situations of co-location, it assists communication through face-to-face conversations.

- It offers continuous attention to XP.

- It adds simplicity.

4.2. Explain Scrum overview

- Scrum is a processed framework meant to help teams develop projects in an iterative, incremental manner. The process is organized in cycles of work called *Sprints*.

- These cycles do not last more than four weeks each (usually two weeks) and they are *timeboxed*. This means they end on a specific date whether the work has been completed or not. They are never extended.

- At the beginning of each Sprint, the team chooses one of the project's tasks from a prioritized list. They agree on a common goal of what they believe they can deliver at the completion of the Sprint, something that is tangible and realistic. During the Sprint, no additional tasks should be added.

- The team meets every day to review their progress and adjust the steps needed to complete the remaining work.

- At the end of the Sprint, the team reviews the work cycle with the stakeholders and shows the end product. With the feedback they get, they plan the next Sprint.

- Scrum emphasizes on obtaining a working product at the completion of each Sprint. When talking about software, this means a system that is integrated, tested, end-user documented, and shippable.

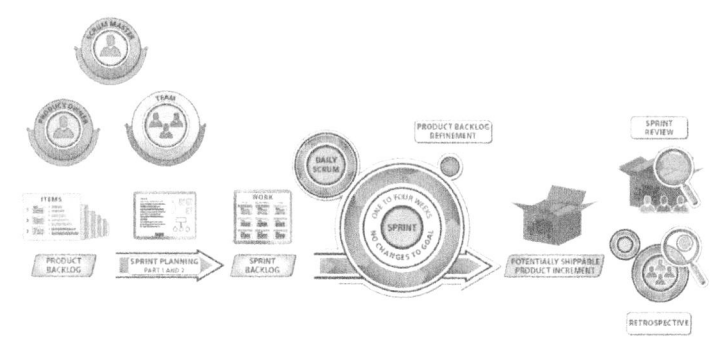

Figure 1.18 : SCRUM Process in a nutshell

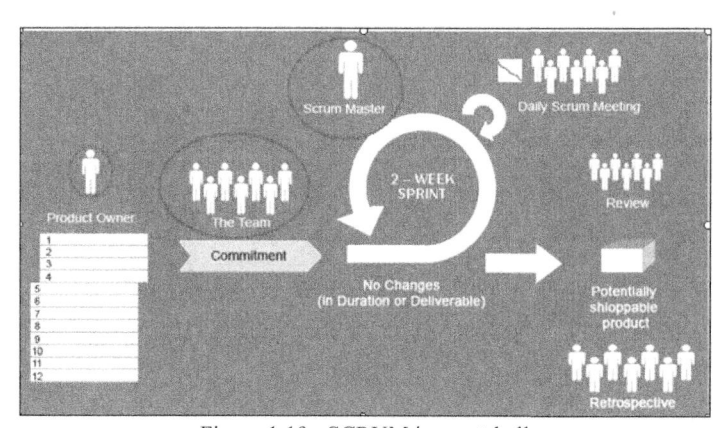

Figure 1.19 : SCRUM in a nutshell

4.3. What are the five phases of risk management?

1. Risk identification
2. Risk categorization
3. Risk response
4. Risk review
5. Risk closure

4.4. What are the main tools used in a Scrum project?

- JIRA

- Rally

- Version One

- Azure

4.5. How can a Scrum Master track the progress of a Sprint?

Scrum Masters can track the Sprint progress by using the Sprint burndown chart. The vertical axis shows the new estimate of work remaining while the horizontal one shows the number of Sprints.

This graph shows, each day, a new estimate of how much work remains until the Team is finished.

Product Backlog Item	Sprint Task	Volunteer	Initial Estimate of Effort	1	2	3	4	5	6
As a buyer, I want to place a book in a shopping cart	modify database	Sanjay	5	4	3	0	0	0	
	create webpage (UI)	Jing	3	3	3	2	0	0	
	create webpage (Javascript logic)	Tracy & Sam	2	2	2	2	1	0	
	write automated acceptance tests	Sarah	5	5	5	5	5	0	
	update buyer help webpage	Sanjay & Jing	3	3	3	3	3	0	
	...								
Improve transaction processing performance	merge DCP code and complete layer-level tests		5	5	5	5	5	5	
	complete machine order for pRank		3	3	8	8	8	8	
	change DCP and reader to use pRank http API		5	5	5	5	5	5	
	...	...	...						
		Total	50	49	48	44	43	34	

Figure 1.20 : Tracking Progress during Sprint – Example 1

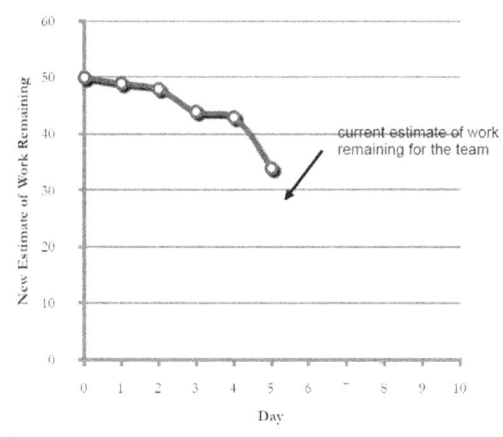

Figure 1.21 : Sprint Burndown Chart – Example 1

		Hours of Work Remaining on Each Day of the Sprint									
Task	Task Owner	Day 1	Day 2	Day 3	Day 4	Day 5	Day 6	Day 7	Day 8	Day 9	Day 10
Configure database and space IDs for Trac	Sanjay	4	4	3	1	0					
Use test data to tune the learning and action model	Jing	2	2	2	2	1					
Setup a cart server code to run as apache server	Philip	3	3	5	2	0					
Implement pre-Login Handler	Tracy	3	3	3	3	3					
Merge DCP code and complete layer-level tests	Jing	5	5	2	2	2					
Complete machine order for pRank	Jing	4	4	3	3	3					
Change DCP and reader to use pRank http API	Tracy	3	3	0	0	0					
	Total	50	48	44	43	34					

Figure 1.22 : Tracking Progress during Sprint – Example 2

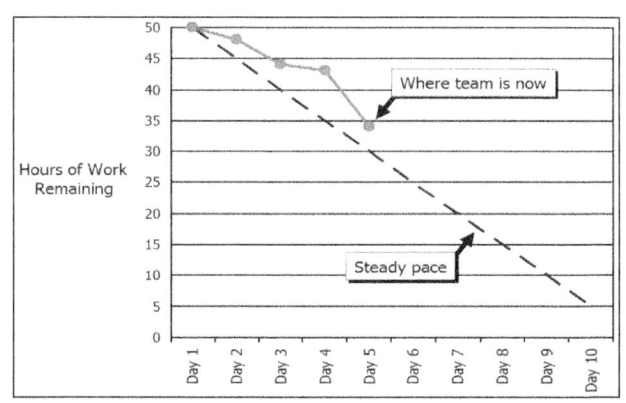

Figure 1.23 : Sprint Burndown Chart – Example 2

4.6. What is timeboxing in Scrum?

Timeboxing means allotting a fixed unit of time for an activity. The unit of time is called a *time box*. The maximum length of a time box should be 15 minutes.

4.7. Is cancelling a Sprint possible? Who can cancel a Sprint?

A Sprint can be cancelled before the Sprint timebox limit ends. Only the Product Owner can cancel the sprint.

4.8. How is estimation in a Scrum project done? What are the techniques used for estimation?

Estimation in a Scrum project is done using relative Agile estimation techniques:

a. The T-shirt estimation technique
b. The planning poker estimation technique
c. The estimation by analogy technique
d. The disaggregation estimation technique

4.9. What are the roles involved in the Scrum framework?

A Scrum framework has three roles:

a. Scrum Master
b. Product Owner
c. Development team

5.0. What is the difference between change management in a Waterfall and in an Agile Scrum?

In Waterfall, change management is based on the change management plan, the change tracker and the release plan based on which the consultants deliver their work.

In agile there is no change management plan. Based on definition of ready product backlog, team is grooming Sprint backlog and delivering their work.

5.1. What is the purpose of a daily Scrum?

The daily Scrum meeting is for the team. It helps them self-organize towards their sprint commitment and set the context for the next day's work.

Daily SCRUM Meeting

Who Attends?	Development Team participation is mandatory. Product Owner or SCRUM Master participation is optional. But they can attend it based on the request.
When Happens?	Every day of the Sprint. **Choose a time that works for everyone.** It is held at the same time and place every day to reduce complexity.
Time-box	Maximum length of 15 minutes or less.
Input	Sprint Goal and Sprint Backlog
Outcome	Plan for next 24 hours and List of impediments (if any).
General Questions discussed	During the meeting, each Team member explains: - What did he do yesterday that helped the team meet the Sprint Goal? - What will he do today to help the team meet the Sprint Goal? - Does he see any impediments that prevent him or the team from meeting the Sprint Goal? In a nutshell, it's interactive bilateral communication to understand: - Where the Development Team is in terms of achieving Sprint Goal? - How Development Team can do differently, i.e., how Development Team can change the tactics to achieve more towards Sprint Goal in order to produce releasable product increment? - Development team tracks sprint roadmap progress based on Sprint Burndown / Burn up Charts where Effort **Unit Story Points** is plotted against Sprint number of day.
Generic Challenges	- The team is all working on separate things, no common Sprint Goal. - 'Mini-waterfall' syndrome i.e., cross dependency. - Self-organisation is a buzz word that has little practical meaning for the team. - All Teams are not in sync in case of distributed teams. - Mobile Friendly Cloud enabled cost optimum tool is missing for 24/7/365

	customer support. - JIRA Tool has many limitations.
Daily Scrum Meeting Best Practices	- Choose a time that works for everyone. - Always focus on outcome rather than output. - Always focus on achieving Sprint Goal. - Keep stand-up efficient and keep everyone engaged, avoid making duplicate conversation and make the discussion short and crispy. Rotate who keeps time to make sure everyone is accountable and invested. If everything is fine, you may make it less than 15 minutes. Remember it's a problem identification meeting, but it is not problem solving meeting. - Stand in a *circle* near your desks. - Review and update sprint backlog every day. - No side conversations. - Meeting rules notice. - Same time and same place every day. Make effective use of **Daily Scrum Meeting (DSM) Tool**, JIRA Tool, Stride + stand-up for distributed teams. **DSM)**APPLICATION SOLVES MANY PRACTICAL ISSUES THAT EVERY PROJECT EXPERIENCES IN THE DEVELOPMENT STAGE. Manage your workload, communicate with your team, and celebrate success.
Benefits of Daily Scrum Meeting	- Improves communication within the Team. - Identifies impediments, if any, in order to facilitate an early removal of the same, so as to minimize impact on the Sprint. - Highlights and promote quick decision-making. - Improves the team's level of knowledge.
Tools / techniques used	DSM Tool, JIRA Tool, Stride + stand-up for distributed teams. Telemetry technique is used to measure

	value. Dot Voting and Bottom-Up facilitation techniques are used for decision making.
Summary	Update and coordination by continuous inspection and adaptation of the sprint backlog, it's a planning event, not status tracking events.

5.2. What do you understand by the term scope creep? How do you prevent it from happening?

If the requirements are not properly defined at the start and new features are added to the product already being built, a scope creep occurs. To prevent it:

1. The requirements must be clearly specified.
2. The project progress must be monitored.
3. Effective grooming of sprint backlog must be done.

5.3. What are the most common risks in a Scrum project?

1. A scope creep
2. Timeline issues
3. Budget issues

5.4. What do you understand by Minimum Viable Product in Scrum?

A **Minimum Viable Product** (**MVP**) is a product with the minimum required features to be shown to the stakeholders and be eligible to ship for production.

5.5. What is the major advantage of using Scrum?

Early feedback, as well as the production of the Minimal Viable Product to the stakeholders, would be the main advantages of using it.

5.6. What does DoD mean? How can this be achieved?

Definition of Done is formed by a list of tasks that define the work's quality. It is used to decide whether an activity from the Sprint backlog is completed.

General

- Create the feature branch and push the changes according to above recommendations
- Code produced (all 'to do' items in code completed)
- Code commented, checked in and run against current version in source control
- Peer reviewed (or produced with pair programming) and meeting development standards
- Builds without errors - check Sonar
- Unit tests written and passing
- Deployed to system test environment and passed system tests
- Passed **User Acceptance Testing (UAT)** and signed off as meeting requirements
- Any build/deployment/configuration changes implemented/documented/communicated
- Relevant documentation/diagrams produced and/or updated
- Remaining hours for task set to zero and task closed

AEM
- Component name are the same in the codebase and in the dialog
- TouchUI dialog is defined for the component
- Component lifecycle (add component, edit dialog, activate for publish) is tested:
    I. Default-values are implemented where necessary and tested.
    II. Component is tested in the targeted browsers.
    III. Changing component properties should not break the current and other components.
- Sonar test passed by Java code
- Test coverage level is covered
- Component / feature has been tested on publish instance (with a dispatcher)
- Sample content for the component has been added
- Clients for the component has been updated with css and js files

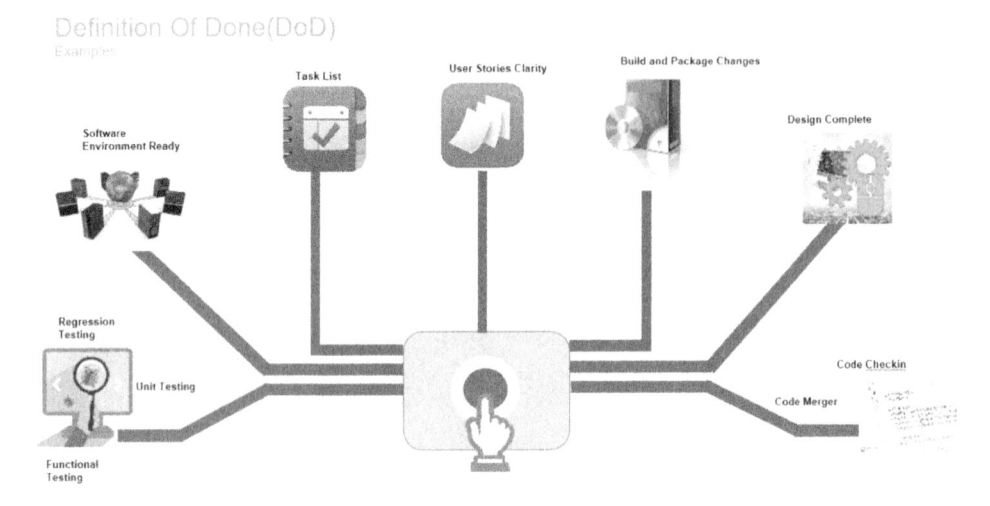

Figure 1.24 : Definition Of Done – Example 1

Sample Definition of Done

- Code produced (all 'to do' items in code completed)
- Code commented, checked in and run against current version in source control
- Peer reviewed (or produced with pair programming) and meeting development standards
- Builds without errors
- Unit tests written and passing
- Deployed to system test environment and passed system tests
- Passed **User Acceptance Testing (UAT)** and signed off as meeting requirements
- Any build / deployment / configuration changes are implemented / documented / communicated
- Relevant documentation / diagrams produced and / or updated
- Remaining hours for task set to zero and task closed

Definition of Done

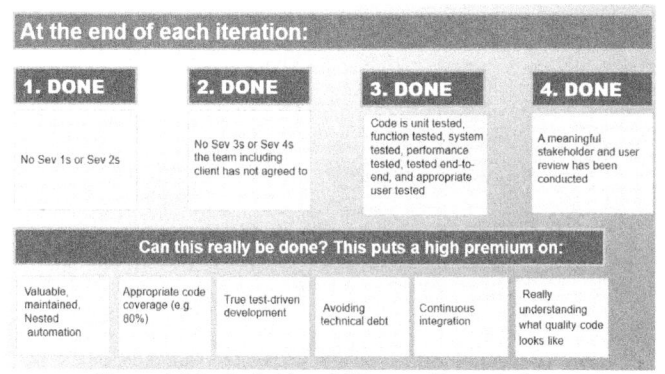

1. DONE	2. DONE	3. DONE	4. DONE
No Sev 1s or Sev 2s	No Sev 3s or Sev 4s the team including client has not agreed to	Code is unit tested, function tested, system tested, performance tested, tested end-to-end, and appropriate user tested	A meaningful stakeholder and user review has been conducted

Can this really be done? This puts a high premium on:

| Valuable, maintained, Nested automation | Appropriate code coverage (e.g. 80%) | True test-driven development | Avoiding technical debt | Continuous integration | Really understanding what quality code looks like |

Figure 1.25 : Definition Of Done – Example 2

5.7. What is velocity in Scrum?

Velocity calculates the total effort the team has put into a Sprint. The number is obtained by adding all the story points from the previous Sprint. It is a guideline for the team to understand the number of stories they can do in a Sprint.

5.8. List out the disadvantages of Scrum

- Daily Scrum meetings require frequent reviews and substantial resources.
- A successful project relies on the maturity and dedication of the whole team.
- The uncertainty of the product, the changes, and frequent product delivery remain present during the Scrum cycle.
- It depends on a significant change.

5.9. Scrum phases and processes

Scrum Phases and Processes

Initiate	Plan & Estimate	Implement	Review & Retrospect	Release
Create Project Vision	Create User Stories	Create Deliverables	Demonstrate and Validate Sprint	Ship Deliverables
Identify Scrum Master & Stakeholder(s)	Estimate User Stories	Conduct Daily Standup	Retrospect Sprint	Retrospect Project
Form Scrum Team	Commit User Stories	Groom Prioritized Product Backlog		
Develop Epics	Identify Tasks			
Create Prioritized Product Backlog	Estimate Tasks			
Conduct Release Planning	Create Sprint Backlog			

Figure 1.26 : SCRUM phases and processes in a nutshell

6.0. SCRUM Flow

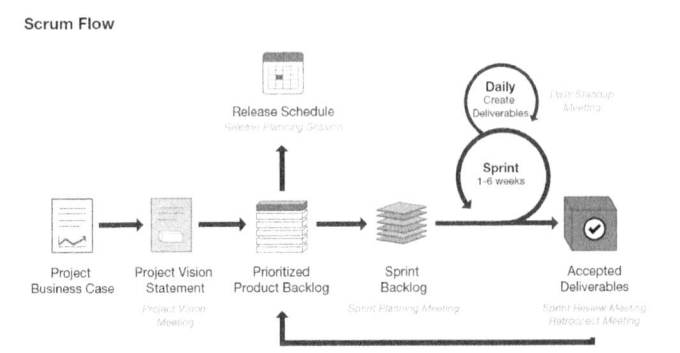

Figure 1.27 : SCRUM Process Flow in a nutshell

6.1. Definition of Ready

Having a **Definition of Ready** means that stories must be immediately actionable.

Sample Definition of Ready

- User Story is clear
- User Story is testable
- User Story is feasible
- User Story defined
- User Story Acceptance Criteria defined
- User Story dependencies identified
- User Story sized by development team
- Scrum Team accepts user experience artefacts
- Performance criteria identified, where appropriate
- Scalability criteria identified, where appropriate
- Security criteria identified, where appropriate
- Person who will accept the User Story is identified
- Team has a good idea what it will mean to Demo the User Story

6.2. PDCA Cycle in SCRUM

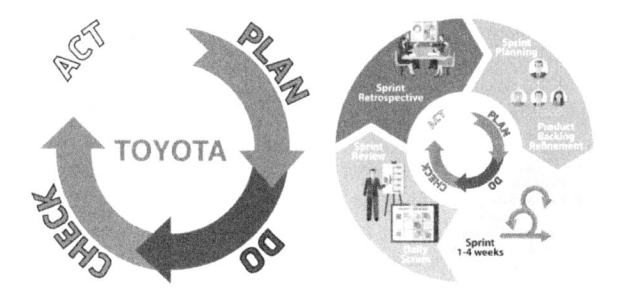

Figure 1.28 : PDCA cycle in SCRUM

6.3. Why SCRUM Master is a Servant Leader?

SCRUM Master is system thinker. He / she has more value to:

    a. Empathy

    b. Active listening

    c. Persuasion

    d. Conflict resolution

e. Effective questioning skills

f. Grooming others

g. Self-awareness

h. Continuous learning

i. Credibility

6.4. What factor decides you whether you will do Project in SCRUM way?

When in complex environment we have specified timebox and definition of ready in Product backlog for our development work, i.e., where volume of work is predictable we can use SCRUM.

6.5. SCRUM real life issue

Suppose, tomorrow, two SCRUM team members took sick leave. You are supposed to give delivery after two weeks. You are following waterfall methodology. What you should do? All other team members are very busy and primary (P1) and secondary resource (P2) concept is not there.

We will check from the resource that whether anybody is doing any low priority work where delivery date is far later. So, we will ask them to do High priority work. We will ask them to keep aside the low priority work.

6.6. What did you do as SCRUM Master to prevent scope creep?

Where agile methods (like scrum) in itself will reduce the risk of scope creep through iterations as well as refinement of user stories only for the relevant sprint, i.e., effectively grooming sprint backlog from definition of ready Product backlog, the issues may still apply within the shorter lifecycles. Hence, scope management is still necessary and the principles are still applicable.

6.7. Example of one positive risk in your SCRUM project

We are finishing second sprint well ahead of delivery schedule.

6.8. Example of one negative risk in your SCRUM project

The product owner on the project quitting the job, even if his backup is not ready.

6.9. What are the main reasons for crashing schedule in your SCRUM project?

Delivering products well ahead of project milestone date.

7.0. Can we use DevOps in your SAP scrum project?

Yes,

By using ABAPGIT and Jenkins as per latest update from SAP TechEd.

7.1. In SCRUM, where customers are involved?

In sprint review and in sprint planning, customers are involved.

7.2. What makes daily SCRUM a waste of time?

a. The team members are doing multi-tasking. They are not in sync with each other's. They put more stress on individual performance. They put less importance on team work.
b. The team members are working on SCRUMBUT project. It is not 100% Scrum. It is not 100% waterfall.
c. The team members are geographically distributed in multiple countries. Each team member is not aware of other's work. They put less importance on self-organized team.

7.3. What techniques are used in daily SCRUM?

Dot voting and bottom up facilitation techniques are used for decision making.

7.4. Who attends daily SCRUM?

- Development team participation is mandatory.
- Product owner or scrum master participation is optional.

7.5. What are the differences between Product backlog and Sprint backlog?

Product Backlog	Sprint Backlog
• The Requirements	• Individuals signs up for work of their own choosing
• A list of all desired work on the project	• Estimated work remaining is updated daily
• Ideally expressed such that each item has value to the users or customers of the product	• Any team member can add, delete, change the Sprint backlog
• Prioritized by the Product owner (MoSCoW rule)	• If work is unclear, define a sprint backlog item with a larger amount of time and break it down later
• Reprioritized at the start of each Sprint	• Update work remaining as more becomes known

7.6. MoSCoW Prioritization technique

Letter	Stands for	Which means
M	Must Have	• Minimum set of essential requirements, without which the system would be useless (MMF) • All of these requirements must be satisfied.
S	Should Have	• Important requirements for which there is a short-term work-around. The system is useful without them.

		• These requirements can be included in the initial project scope, but may be removed from the project scope to accommodate changed requirements.
C	Could Have	• These requirements are valuable and nice-to-have, but can easily be left out of the solution. • These requirements may be left out of the initial scope of the release in order to accommodate a time constraint.
W	Would have/Won't have	• Time-permitting. • As changes to requirements or project progress dictates, lower priority requirements may be removed from the scope of the project.

7.7. Scrum master certification exam sample questions

You need to attend two days' workshop to have idea on scrum master certification questions.

Is it difficult to crack a Scrum Master interview?

No. You need to have atleast two years of hands-on scrum experience.

What are the primary skills that a recruiter looks into?

Servant leadership

Latest updates for interviewees

From Agile scrum blogs you can get it.

7.8. Important tips to prepare for an interview
1. Review the most commonly asked questions, listed above.
2. Do some previous research on the company.
3. Find a way to develop a connection with the interviewer.
4. Be positive and be confident.
5. End the interview on a positive note.

7.9. Conclusion

Now that the Scrum Master's profession is in such demand, this career ranks 10th on the list of the most promising jobs. A professional Scrum Master salary ranges from $107,280 to $136,748 per annum. Having a certification adds value to an applicant's résumé.
There are many questions during an interview that do not have a right or wrong answer. It all depends on each organization and the applicant's perspective when resolving the situation. Hence, one should also be prepared for general questions.

Meta description: Preparing to clear your Scrum interview? Here's the article that exposes you to 100 PLUS most commonly asked Scrum Master interview questions and the best answers.

8.0. Common Agile Product Development Myths

Myth #1: Isn't Agile Just for Software Development?

But actually, because agile works with all kinds of products—software is only one of them.

This is an intriguing myth because Scrum is the oldest agile approach and Scrum's origins are in physical product development. Some of the original Scrum projects were photocopiers, a Honda car, and cameras.

Agile these days is used for all forms of product development, from physical products to cloud-based **software-as-a-service (SaaS)**.

But beyond product development (both hardware and software), agile is being used successfully by:

- Marketing teams to plan and execute campaigns
- Attorneys to manage cases and workload
- Organizational transformation efforts, in particular when transitioning to agile
- Senior leadership teams to manage their organizations
- Families for improving time together
- Couples planning weddings
- And, of course, many more

Myth #2: Is It True That Managers Have No Role in Agile?

Not True always.

In all the years, I've worked with agile and agile organizations, not one has decided to fire all managers. Yes, some managers have moved into the more focused roles of Scrum Master or product owner, but there is still a role for management in agile.

Myth #3: Can't stakeholders introduce change whenever they want?

Not True always.

If the change is introduced at the right time, there may be little or no cost. Introduced at the wrong time, though, and there is a cost.

Being agile cannot eliminate all costs of stakeholders introducing change. However, good agile teams can reduce the cost of change regardless of when the change is introduced. Common ways of doing this are as follows:

- short iterations

- small product backlog items
- Finishing each product backlog item as quickly as possible, usually by minimizing the number of items being worked on concurrently.

None of this is to say that teams shouldn't welcome appropriate changes. Some stakeholder-requested changes can be very important. But, the benefit of making each change needs to be assessed against the cost of changing and that cost is not always zero.

Myth #4: Doesn't everyone need to be a generalist on an Agile team?

This is entirely false.

Agile teams don't need everyone to have every skill. Instead, what agile teams need is to value any individuals who do possess skills in multiple disciplines.

Having a few team members with multiple skills helps manage the balance of types of work. That is, sometimes the team needs more testing capacity.

But this can be accomplished on most teams even if a few team members are truly specialists and adept at only one discipline.

Myth #5: I've heard that Agile teams don't (or can't) plan.

Most good agile teams do plan but that planning is often less visible than on traditional projects because agile teams don't have an upfront planning phase.

Instead, good agile teams conduct planning as a series of smaller, recurring activities that ensure their plans always reflect the realities of the current situation.

In this way, teams develop plans the same way they develop products: by inspecting and adapting.

Consider a traditional team with analysis, design, coding and testing phases. If lucky, that team may delay committing to a plan until the end of the design phase. But at that point, this team has no idea how fast they are at coding and testing—they haven't done any of those activities yet.

In contrast, an agile team turns the entire build into multiple iterations. Each iteration includes a little analysis, design, coding, and testing. This gives the agile team more and earlier insight into how quickly it can turn ideas into new features.

Myth #6: Don't Agile teams create products with no architectural plan?

It's time to bust our final myth: the myth that agile teams don't architect or design their products.

Agile teams definitely design their products. But, in the same way they plan incrementally, agile teams architect and design incrementally. This allows them to inspect and adapt their architectures and designs so they become the best possible.

This means there is no upfront phase during which all architectural decisions are made. Instead the architecture of a product emerges over time.

This occurs by technical team members focusing first on any aspects of a product they consider risky. For example, if delivering a product with the needed throughput will be challenging, the team and product owner would elect to work on functionality early on that reduces that risk.

In this way, the emergent architecture of an agile product is also intentional. The architecture doesn't just show up one day. It emerges gradually and guided by the intent of the technical team members.

This means that agile products do possess an underlying architecture. But decisions about that architecture are made as needed through the course of the project rather than being made entirely at the start of the project.

9.0. Three Types of "Scrum Teams"

Type 1: Groups that try to do Scrum
Most Dangerous

- Low-level of task interdependence.
- Do not need to work together as a team (Context does not require teamwork).
- Forced to do Scrum because that is what everyone else is doing.
- Group members hate Scrum because it does not work. How could it?
- Retrospectives add little to no value—Take seven random people in a bar and have them conduct a retrospective on the work they did not do together.

Vital Flaw: Thinking that method precedes context.

Sports analogy: Wrestlers

Type 2: Scrum "Teams"

Characteristics

- People who have a high-level of task interdependence but do not know how to work together as a team.
- They do Scrum things and worry about buffer, writing user stories, and happiness metrics.
- Think sending an email builds situational awareness and is part of closed-loop communication.
- Spend time talking about the differences between themes, initiatives, epics, and stories.
- Retrospectives change frequently and tend to focus on what went well, what didn't, and so on.
- Planning sessions and the daily Scrum look nothing alike.
- Members and coaches hold several certifications and use phrases such as: *That's not agile* and *Let's self-organize and move these chairs toward the wall so we can...*
- Lacks agility but claim they are agile.
- Managers in the organization consider the team to be *Agile* because they are either (1) trained in Scrum or (2) are doing Scrum.
- Have a *me* attitude.
- Low-level of employee engagement.

- May occasionally achieve a 2X improvement in velocity.

Vital Flaw: Assumption that people with high-technical skills or advanced education know how to team.

Sports Analogy: 2002-2004 USA Men's Basketball Dream Team (**Hint**: they lost to teams that knew how to play together)

Type 3: Teams that use Scrum
Significant Competitive Advantage

Characteristics

- Two or more people who work interdependently, adaptively, and dynamically towards a shared and valued goal/objective/mission (This is actually the definition of a team)
- Improve team interactions daily
- Know how to mitigate cognitive biases
- Each member can lead any event
- Members display fallibility
- Prioritized Teamwork training over Framework training (Scrum)
- Practice closed-loop communication
- Challenge each other's assumptions
- Detect weak signals
- Have a *we* attitude
- Scrum used to help prioritize work, build a cadence, and create a container
- Scrum is a force multiplier
- Teams know how to separate decisions from outcomes
- Follow the 60/40 rule in retrospectives: 60% focus on teamwork (Teaming skills) and 40% on task work
- Not uncommon to see a 4X to 16X improvement in velocity

Vital Flaw: Waiting! Waiting is failure!

Sports Analogy: All Blacks, New England Patriots, 1980 USA Men's Olympic Hockey Team.

Bottom line: If you want to create agility, prioritize Teamwork over Frameworks.
Give more stress on team outcome achieved rather than efforts spent.

10.0. Agile Budget Management

Agile budget calculation is very hot buzzword now. Here, you need to calculate your labor costs, non-labor costs, NFR costs apart from calculating your labor costs for functional/technical requirements.

How is your budget being allocated today?

• Top down decision by leader/leaders

• Same budget as last year with small changes

- Start from scratch each year aligning resources to priorities

- I don't know

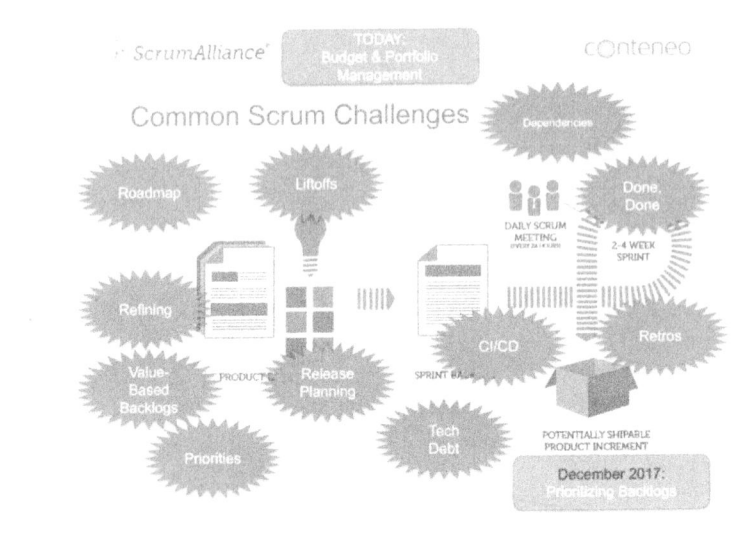

Figure 1.29 : SCRUM – Common challenges

Image source: https://www.scrumalliance.org

In Agile we are getting big business requirements in terms of Epics which are combination of many related user stories.

- Prepare and estimate the project requirements using planning oker
- Determine the team's velocity

Prepare and estimate the project requirements using planning poker

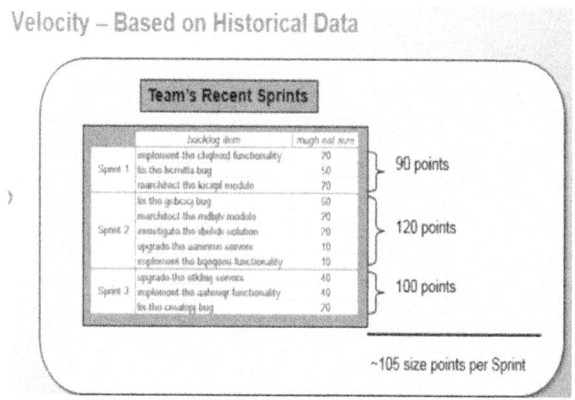

Figure 1.29 : Calculation of Velocity per Sprint - Example

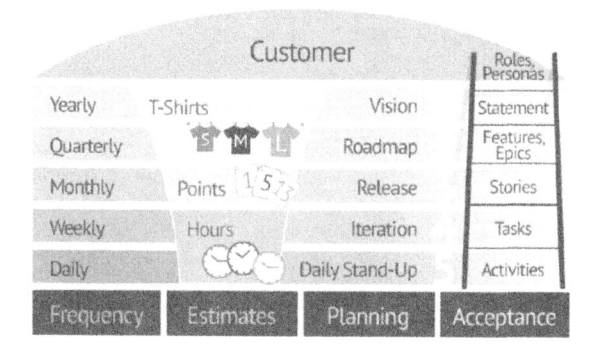

Figure 1.30 : Different types of planning in SCRUM

Image source: https://www.scrumalliance.org

Reference – Go to the following URL to have detailed case study.

https://www.linkedin.com/pulse/agile-budget-calculation-utopia-worldwide-across/

11.0. Agile Contract Management

Time and Material (T&M) type contracts are a good fit for Agile engagements.

Fixed Price / Fixed Capacity (FPFC) contract is most suitable for Agile whereas a contract with Fixed Price / Fixed scope must be avoided.

We have noticed that most clients know only a small percentage of their complete requirements at the start of any new project. This is more so for an application / site development and we observed something very similar in platform / technology migration situations as well. Later, most customers wanted to add new features as well which makes it somewhat like a new development. Asking them to define the priorities is almost impossible. What we have tried here are various things (in case of fixed price).

For risk & Impact / analyse and design phase we have put T&M contract, for Build & testing till UAT we have put *Fixed Price – 70/30 mode* which puts 30% of the revenue on a penalty mode if there is any slippage in timeline or quality. Closely work with client to create contract – defining the prerequisites and exit criteria. After UAT till Go-Live and support / hypercare phase we have put T&M contract.

Reference – Go to the below URL to have detailed case study.

https://www.linkedin.com/pulse/agile-scrum-contract-best-practices-sudipta-malakar-csp/

1. We try and explain that any changes to the requirements will swap out an equal sized but lower priority requirement. Thus the client keeps the budget in check and has the flexibility even late in the project life cycle to add / remove requirements.

2. We try and have a T & M requirement phase where the Product Backlog is frozen (maybe 80%) and then give a fixed bid quote (with appropriate assumptions and margins for error).

3. We have clauses in the contract where we say that project estimates will be revisited at specified intervals and all estimations etc. will be transparent.

While these measures have helped, it really depends a lot on the client's understanding of Agile and willingness to collaborate. Otherwise it's always a tough and bumpy ride, especially in Agile projects.

Firm fixed price	Target price	Cost plus	Time and materials
- Fixed specification - Fixed price and date - Changes with a fee - Risk to Supplier	- Fixed specification - Fixed date - Target price - Negotiated profit for the Supplier above target price - Shared risk, shared economic opportunity	- Target specification - Target date - Customer pays Supplier's cost plus profit margin - Risk mostly shifted to Customer	- No complete specification - Price based on rate - Ends as specified by Customer - Risk shifted to Customer

Figure 1.31 : Different types of Agile Contracts
Image Source: PMI PMBOK

Other popular contract types include paying by features contract, time and materials contract, fixed price and fixed scope contract, and fixed profit contract.

Thorup and Jensen (2009) explain in their paper the option of Graduated Fixed Price (see Exhibit3)

Project Completion	Total Fee	Graduated Rate
Finish Early	$87,000	$117/hour
Finish On-Time	$100,000	$100/hour
Finish Late	$113,000	$90/hour

Figure 1.32 : Contract - Illustration
Image Source: PMI PMBOK

12.0. Agile – Key Takeaways

By agile, we mean a number of things:

- Enhanced flexibility
- Empowering employees to work where, when and how they choose
- Iterative delivery of projects
- Co-ownership of projects with the client / customer
- The opportunity to adapt ways of working and processes as objectives change and move on throughout a project lifecycle.

Which of these descriptions best applies to the project management function within the organization?

- Established processes in place, with ongoing improvements and innovations introduced, based on feedback from monitoring and evaluation.

Senior managers are actively keen that the **Portfolio Program Manager (PPM)** function becomes more strategic (e.g. has more tangible and identifiable impact on overall business goals and finances).

Agile is a value driven approach, not plan driven.

A plan driven, project focused, approach is what we learned when we got our PMP's. Everything is planned up front. Requirements are fixed, and cost and schedule are estimated. We then report status based on how the project is doing compared to the plan.

When it comes to software development, we know a plan driven approach is flawed. Yet, many companies continue to use it. Why? Why do we punish project teams for being over budget or behind schedule when we know it's the process that's broken?

We need to shift our mindset from project focus, to product focus.

Product focus is a value driven, adaptive process. It doesn't punish teams for change. It anticipates change and even welcomes it.

In a value driven approach, cost is fixed, and features are estimated. It's the reverse of a plan driven approach. Investment is made at the product level, not a project level. People are dedicated to teams, and the teams stay intact.

It's not for small tech firms only. Target, for example, has completely shifted to a product focus model. They get it, and they're not alone. Many large companies are organizing cross functional teams around products. They are bringing IT and business people together to focus on delivering business outcomes.

If your company is going Agile, ask yourself, are you ready to move on from traditional project management? Are you ready to no longer have a PMO? Are you ready to change? If yes, then it's time to embrace a product focused mindset. If no, then continue using waterfall, but don't call it Agile.

Bottom line: If you want to create agility, prioritize Teamwork over Frameworks.

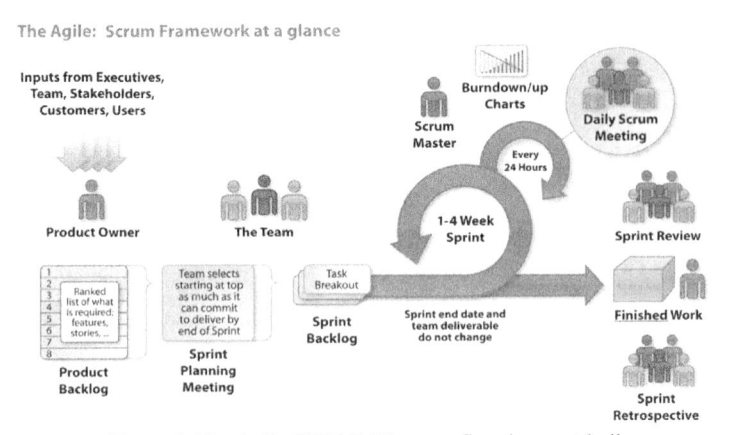

Figure 1.32 : Agile SCRUM Process flow in a nutshell

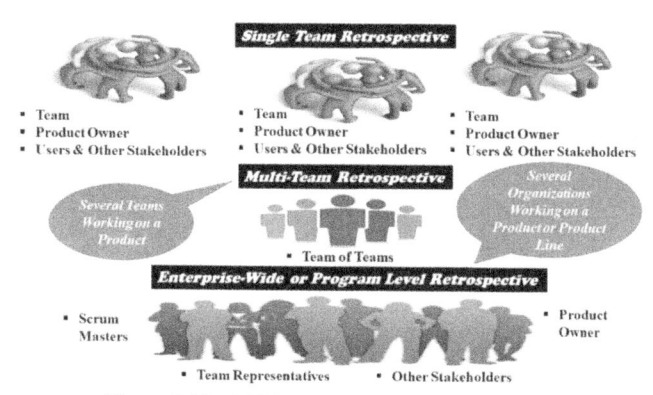

Figure 1.33 : SCRUM Retrospective types

In today's development world, every company always tries to provide the best-ever solutions to its clients. In this process, most companies opt for the agile software development process because by using this, they are able to develop and deliver the product that clients need at any time. Also, in this process, any type of changes or new requirements can be easily handled as a new feature of the product. So, in this article, we will discuss the Agile methodology and why this process is very important in the software development industry.

History of Agile

As a general concept, the Agile Software Development process was first introduced in 2001 when the Agile Manifesto was brought into life with some basic software development methods. But, in fact, before 2001, people already started working in an Agile fashion. In those days, software developers started working with both old and new ideas and started trying to mix these ideas to create a proper combination of methodology which would help them or their team to develop the product. People who create these types of methodologies, try to create a framework on the basis of these methodologies so that they can spread this idea among other teams or the company to help them in tough situations. This is when several frameworks like Scrum, Extreme Programming, Feature-Driven Development etc. came into the picture.

In 2001, 17 people held a meeting at a ski resort in Snowbird, Utah to discuss the similarities of different software development processes, and declared a common manifesto for Agile Software Development. Actually, Agile is a mindset according to the Agile Manifesto. The Agile Manifesto basically provides some basic values and principles which provide us guidance on how to create and respond to the changes, along with teaching us how to deal with uncertainty.

For 2001 until now, the Agile process has evolved and presented a model to adapt to changes in the world. In simple words, the Agile Software Development process is a group of methods and principles related to software development. In this development process, all the requirements and solutions for the software development are evolved through a collaborative effort of self-organizing and cross-functional teams.

WHAT IS AGILE?

Agile is a methodology or mindset which consists of several iterative and incremental software development methodologies. Agile always has the ability to create and respond to change. The Agile methodology involves continuous planning, testing, integration, and feedback from the stakeholders or clients throughout the life cycle of the software. The main objective of these models is to increase team involvement, and also make quick decisions as per the situations.

Agile methodology is mainly designed and developed to avoid common development issues during the software development life cycle and increase the overall efficiency of the development team. Agile always offers a lightweight framework which helps the development team in dealing with a constantly functional and technical landscape and also focuses on continuous delivery. With the help of this process, the company can reduce the overall risk associated with software development.

So, in a single sentence, the developments performed using Agile methodologies are normally developed and built iteratively and incrementally. In this methodology, a company can produce or deliver a quality product in less time and improve customer satisfaction at the end.

WHY CHOOSE AGILE?

In today's world, technologies are changing at a much faster pace than earlier, which requires the software development companies to work in a fast-paced changing environment. Since companies are developing solutions in an ever-changing environment, it is not always possible to gather all the requirement and clarifications at the time of starting the development. And obviously, without these requirement studies, it becomes very difficult to implement any conventional software model, like the Waterfall Model which totally depends on the complete specification of the requirements, designing and testing of the system.

These types of models will not be able to be geared towards rapid software development process. As a result, these conventional software development models fail to deliver the required product. Now, this is the situation where the Agile Model can rescue us from this type of situation since the Agile Model is actually specially designed to tackle these types of situation in this rapidly changing environment of software development and also support the incremental development for enhancement of the products.

The basic principles of the Agile Methodologies which are required to be understood to implement Agile in any company as a part of the Software Development Life Cycle are as follows:

1. Top priority is the satisfaction of the customer which can be obtained by early and continuous product delivery.
2. This process always accepts any changes in the requirement, even at the end position of the development.
3. It can deliver working product frequently, with the duration of a couple of weeks to a couple of months.
4. In the process, working software is the only primary measurement of the progress.
5. Using this process, anybody can achieve the most efficient and effective method of transferring information within the development team along with a face-to-face conversation.

Benefits of Agile process

So, once the company has decided to use the Agile Methodology, they must be aware of the benefits which can be obtained using Agile Methodology. Some of the key benefits are as follows:

- A better way of planning
- Proper allocation of resources
- Shorter development cycles
- Easy control of the overall development process
- Can involve the stakeholders in the development analysis process and testing phase
- Always contains clear transparency
- Can be integrated into a systematic plan
- Can predict the feature delivery work
- Easy to predict cost and schedule the work accordingly
- Easy acceptance of any changes within the SDLC
- This process can help improve quality
- Help to collect the current development feedback so that work can be improved in the next increment period

Everything is not good

In Agile Software Development process, everything is not good as expected. There are some issues which can be treated as a disadvantage of the Agile methodology:

- The Agile process is mainly focused on the code work or development work but there is no consideration related to the documentation work required related to the development work.
- In the case of large software development, it is quite impossible to estimate the total costs of the entire project in the initial stage of the development.
- Rapid decisions can be taken by the senior and experienced developers. So, it is quite impossible for an inexperienced or less experienced developer to make the decisions.

SUMMARY

So, Agile is a framework or methodology which helps us to plan or decide how the software development process needs to be carried out. Agile is not a single process or mechanism. It is basically containing a group of methods and best practices according to the Agile Manifesto. But, the Agile process never promises to solve all the problems which are present in the current software industry. This process actually establishes a culture and a mindset where the solution needs to merge. A survey by a reputed firm of over 600+ companies found that most of the companies or organizations are either already adopting the Agile Methodology or will adopt this process. Some of the company like Apple, Microsoft, Amazon etc. are using Agile methodology in their best way.

13. Quiz Session

Questions

1. Which practice does not fall under Technical best practices?

Select the correct answer.
A. Automated build & Continuous Integration
B. Automated Regression Testing
C. Code Review & Rework
D. None of the above

2. Retrospective meetings help us to_____.

Select the correct answer.
A. Identify areas of improvement
B. Recognize team members
C. Inspect and adapt
D. All of the above

3. Sprint backlog is updated by _____.

Select the correct answer.
A. Scrum Master
B. Scrum Team
C. Scrum Product Owner
D. Any of the above

4. Product Owner has to mandatorily participate in Daily Scrum Meeting.

Select the correct answer.
A. Yes
B. No
C. Not required
D. Based on needs

5. Which life cycle model does the Agile method follow:

Select the correct answer.
A. Waterfall model
B. Iterative and Incremental model
C. V-model

D. None of the above

6. Product backlog contains prioritized____ .

Select the correct answer.
A. Epics
B. User stories
C. Epics and user stories
D. None of the above

7. Which of the following roles is not defined by Scrum?

Select the correct answer.
A. Product Owner
B. Project Manager
C. Developer / Tester
D. Scrum Master

Answers

1. D
2. D
3. B
4. D
5. B
6. C
7. B

14.0. Agile – Maturity assessment

Agile Maturity Dashboard

Things to note before you start using this playbook…
- This is a self-assessment tool provided for teams to baseline their maturity with the implementation of their Agile Practices.
- The goal is not to get a maximum score but to identify the practices that need more attention, and areas that can be built upon.
- Use this Playbook to baseline your current practices, identify and implement the improvements, and repeat!
- It is strongly recommended that you use an Agile Coach to conduct you first assessment - there are some terms and practices that need to be explained to be fully understood.
- It is also strongly recommended for this assessment to be conducted involving ALL team members (including any client representatives that may also be part of the team).

How to get started...
- Open the 'Assessment' worksheet
- Fill in the Account / Project Name
- Fill in the Date of Assessment
- For each practice, rate your team from 0-3, based on the rating guidelines provided for each one.
- Place comments where relevant for each practice rating
- Save the spreadsheet
- Print the /Analysis' worksheet and publish it to all team members, and the Program / Project leaders
- Email the updated spreadsheet back to your A/NZ agile coach
- You are done!

What happens next…
- The results are analyzed
- You will receive key findings, and recommendations for improvement
- You will receive a targeted action plan to continuously improve your Agile Practices.
- You can use the results of this assessment to start meaningful discussions in your team's Retrospectives.

A) Assessment:

Agile Practice	How is this practice being used in your project?			Rating (0 - 3)
Stand-Ups	0. Not being used	1. Stand-ups are treated as a status update to the Project Manager or the Iteration Manager (Scrum Master)	2. Stand-ups occur at predefined intervals, and used to synchronise the team efforts.	3. Stand-ups are effective, timeboxed and include highlighting of blockers	2
Task / Progress Wall	0. Not being used	1. Progress wall in place and is the hub of all information for the team and others	2. Progress wall reflects true work status	3. Progress wall is visible in team area and is updated at least daily	1
Big Visible Charts	0. Not being used	1. Some information is displayed visually	2. Most important information displayed visually	3. Team updates visual information on a regular basis	1
Social Contract	0. Not being used	1. Social Contract created by team and displayed visually	2. Team behaviour is checked against agreed contract	3. Social Contract regularly reviewed and adapted	1
Showcase (Iteration / Product Review)	0. Not being used	1. Regular Showcase in place	2. Showcase is consistently attended by team, customers and stakeholders every iteration / release.	3. Showcase content is proudly presented by customers every iteration / release	1
Work Estimation	0. Not being used	1. All work is estimated in term of relative effort and complexity	2. Estimates are created through a team consensus process (planning poker)	3. Estimates are shared with customer and used as the basis for planning	2
Timeboxed Iterations	0. Not being used	1. All iterations are of equal length, less	2. Iterations start and end on the fixed dates, and never	3. Iterations start immediately after the previous one finishes, and the	2

		than 4 weeks in duration.	extended.	scope is adjusted (not the iteration start and end dates) if needed.	
Sustainable Pace	0. Not being used, team members regularly work overtime.	1. Overtime is not planned in the iterations, holidays and other distractions are accounted for when planning the iterations / releases.	2. Scope is adjusted rather than planning to work overtime when needed.	3. The team (not the PM or the Customer) determines the team's velocity, and uses it to plan the releases/iterations so that they can work at a sustainable pace.	1
Success Sliders	0. Not being used	1. Success Sliders agreed between team and customers	2. Success Sliders are used when making decisions	3. All Success Sliders have a clear definition in the context of the work	0
Adaptive Planning	0. Not being used	1. Overall Plan in place and reviewed periodically	2. Overall Plan updated based on evidence of recent progress. Yesterdays' weather (latest velocity) is taken into account.	3. Work practices, team capacity, budget or scope are adjusted to meet agreed objectives	1
Requirements as Stories	0. Not being used	1. Stories are identified using an agreed format	2. Stories are elaborated Just in Time by team including SME	3. Stories use INVEST Model and include acceptance criteria, clear Definition of Done	2
Progress Tracking / Velocity	0. Not being used	1. Progress of work is measured and made highly visible.	2. Points are only awarded when each User Story is 100% complete (according to the Definition of Done).	3. Velocity used for planning / adjusting the future iterations.	1
Retrospectives	0. Not being used	1. Irregularly with no clear actions being agreed	2. Retrospectives occur at least at the end of each iteration, and result in clear	3. The retrospective actions items are treated as part of the next iteration's	2

			prioritised actions.	backlog, and tracked along with other items.	
Co-location	0. Not being used	1. Core team is co-located	2. Core team and SME are co-located	3. Cross-functional team is co-located	1
Requirements Gathering	0. All requirements are fully documented and agreed to towards the start of the project.	1. User Stories are used (instead of detailed Requirements documents) to capture the high-level requirements.	2. Just in time techniques are used to fill in the details of each of the requirements.	3. It is easy to incorporate any changes to the original requirements during the project, as long as the related Users Stories are not already committed into the current iteration.	1
Workshops (wisdom of the crowd)	0. Not being used	1. Workshop only used for significant team activities	2. Workshops are consistently used to achieve consensus	3. All team members take turns in facilitating workshops, utilising a variety of formats / locations.	2
Iteration Planning	0. Not being used	1. Iteration work/activities are planned and agreed	2. Past progress is used as the basis for capacity planning	3. Whole team including SME and customer are involved in Iteration planning sessions	1
Iterative Delivery	0. Not being used	1. Team plans work to be delivered in iterative manner	2. Team knows what determines their collective success and strive towards achieving the points committed to the customer within the iterations	3. Team is consistently delivering all work committed to be delivered within the iteration. There is no work carried over to the future iterations.	1
Frequent Small Releases	0. Not being used	1. Work is planned to provide deliverables at	2. Team breaks up the User Stories to be comfortably	3. Team is able to deliver at least one potentially releasable	1

		regular intervals	delivered within one iteration. There are no User Stories committed into an iteration that need more than one iteration to deliver.	deliverable every iteration.	
Work Prioritisation	0. Not being used	1. Work is prioritised - MoSCoW	2. Whole team including customer prioritise work	3. Priority of work in backlog is regularly reviewed by the customer, based on Business Value.	1
Acceptance TDD	0. Not being used	1. Work is done based on agreed acceptance criteria	2. Acceptance Criteria is used for determining whether the items is done or not.	3. Team is embracing the ATDD way of working.	1
Architecture Design	0. Not being used	1. Incorporating any changes to the original requirements has a huge impact on the architectural design.	2. It is easy to incorporate changes at any stage of the project	3. Just in Time architecture allows the project team to evolve the solution based on changing needs.	0
Agile reporting - Burn (Up/Down)	0. Not being used	1. Burn-Down chart used to measure progress of Iteration	2. Burn-down Chart is highly visible to the team members and others, and updated at daily.	3. Burn-Down chart used to steer progress, used to communicate with customer if there is a need for any adjustments.	0
Agile reporting - Release Planning	0. Not being used	1. A Release Plan (Burn-up) is used to visualise progress of entire scope of work	2. A Release Plan (Burn Up) is accepted by team and stakeholders	3. A Release Plan (Burn Up) is calculated /adjusted from actual work completed every iteration	0
Rotation Model (Cross-Skilling)	0. Not being used	1. Some Team members perform other roles	2. Team members do not stick to their job titles, and most	3. Intentional cross-skilling program in place	1

			team members perform other functional roles.	and no single points of failure exist	
Customer / SME is Available	0. Not being used	1. Customer/SME is available only on request	2. Customer/SME is always available, and they attend all the iteration rituals.	3. Customer/SME is always co-located, has necessary domain knowledge, and seen to be part of the team.	2
Pair Delivery (Pair Programming)	0. Not being used	1. Significant or complex work items are initiated in pairs to agree approach	2. Pair delivery used for majority of implementation	3. Pairs frequently swap within the team (including across-role types) and practice is used to help upskill or on-board team members	1
Test Driven Development	0. Not being used	1. Automated unit tests are implemented and executed before feature / method / behaviour is implemented (RED-GREEN)	2. Implementation is refactored as after feature / method / behaviour is implemented (RED-GREEN-REFACTOR)	3. Other automated test types (integration, functional, acceptance) are implemented using test-first approach	0
Continuous Integration	0. Not being used	1. Continuous Integration builds solution on a regular basis	2. Continuous Integration builds solution and executes automated tests on a regular basis. Failing builds attract immediate attention	3. Continuous Integration provides rapid and visual feedback as changes are committed. Built artefacts are used directly for deployment into test or production environments	1
Continuous Delivery	0. Not being used	1. Team is able to perform frequent releases into production	2. Team has automated the Deployment process to be a one button push.	3. The team is able to deploy to production at a frequency that is demanded by the customers	0
Automated	0. Not being	1. Automated	2. Automated	3. Manual testing	2

Testing	used	tests exist for unit level tests	tests are written for majority test types	only used for exploratory or user acceptance testing with all other tests are automated	
Risk Management	0. Risk Register is not always visible to team and others	1. Each item in the Backlog has a Risk Assessment done	2. The team is encouraged to pull the riskiest items towards the front of the queue for implementation.	3. The Risk Register is highly-visible and is updated at least once every iteration.	0
Testing (including Unit / System / User Acceptance)	0. Not being used (testing is done by client / other vendors)	1. Unit and System testing is performed within the iterations	2. All testing (including UAT) is performed within the iterations	3. Our 'Definition of Done' states that a User Story is complete when the Customer signs-off the 'Acceptance Criteria' on each item within the iteration.	1
Refactoring	0. Not being used	1. Refactoring is incorporated in TDD practices	2. Refactoring is used to address areas of high technical debt/complexity across whole system	3. Technical debt is measured and actively reduced through refactoring	0
Spikes (timeboxed technical investigations)	0. Not being used	1. Spikes are identified during work planning and used to uncover details of complex, high-risk or unestimated requirements	2. Spike timeboxes are strictly observed	3. Spike outcomes are shared with the team (including the customer) and often combined with pair delivery	1
Coding Standards	0. Not being used	1. Coding Standards defined and used	2. Coding Standards exception reporting in place	3. Coding Standards enforced by Continuous Integration	1
Collective Code Ownership	0. Not being used	1. All team members take responsibility for code changes,	2. All team members are confident to make change across the entire	3. The team constantly engages in code reviews and refactor code	1

		quality and maintenance	code base	when necessary.	
Quality	0. The Test Manager is responsible for ensuring the quality of the deliverables.	1. Testers are collectively responsible for ensuring the quality of the deliverables.	2. The team is collectively responsible for defining and ensuring the quality of the deliverables.	3. The Product Owner (customer) defined quality, the team collectively is responsible to ensuring the quality of the deliverables.	2
Team On-Boarding	0. No Team On boarding plan is in place	1. Yes, Team On boarding Process in place	2. Team Ways of Working are clearly defined and introduced to new team members.	3. On-boarding and Off Boarding team members does not drastically impact the team velocity.	2
Business Value Estimates	0. Not being used	1. Features have an associated Bus Value	2. Stories have an identified Bus Value	3. Stories are prioritised based on Business Value points	1
Risk / Issues / Blocker Management	0. Not being used	1. Risks/Issues are visualised on Team Wall	2. Clear Escalation and Mitigation in place	3. Items are reviewed regularly by TEAM and outcomes shared	1
Having Fun	0. Team is too focussed or busy to have fun	1. Team members are enjoying being at work	2. Regular fun (activities) in the team reduced stress and increased creativity.	3. Team members offer new ideas for having fun, and celebrate each other's success.	2
Iteration Management	0. The Scrum Master or the Iteration Manager role does not exist.	1. Project Manager is playing the role of the Iteration Manager	2. Team sees the Iteration Manager (Scrum Master) as a Servant-Leader	3. Team is self-organising, rotating the Iteration Management role amongst the team members	2
Agile Governance	0. Traditional Gantt Charts are used for project reporting	1. Project Steering committee is supportive of the Agile way of Working	2. Project Deliverables are aligned to the Agile Deliverables (as opposed to the traditional milestones / funding)	3. All Project Reporting and Governance are fully aligned to the Agile Way of Working.	2
Self -	0. Most work	1. The Project		3. No one is	1

| Organizing Team | is assigned to the team members by the Iteration Manager or the Project Manager. | manager/ Iteration Manager (Scrum Master) is constantly pushing the team to become self-organising | 2. Most team members volunteer for work. | assigned any work, everyone volunteers for work. | |

B) Analysis:

Agile Practice	Area	Value	How is this practice being used in your project?	Comments
Stand-Ups	Practice	Collaboration	Stand-ups occur at predefined intervals, and used to synchronise the team efforts.	
Task / Progress Wall	Practice	Transparency	Progress wall in place and is the hub of all information for the team and others	
Big Visible Charts	Artefact	Transparency	Some information is displayed visually	
Social Contract	People	Self-Organised	Social Contract created by team and displayed visually	
Showcase (Iteration / Product Review)	Practice	Close to Customer	Regular Showcase in place	
Work Estimation	Practice	Collective Ownership	Estimates are created through a team consensus process (planning poker)	
Timeboxed Iterations	Practice	Timeboxing	Iterations start and end on the fixed dates, and never extended.	

Sustainable Pace	Planning	Sustainable Pace	Overtime is not planned in the iterations, holidays and other distractions are accounted for when planning the iterations / releases.	
Success Sliders	Artefact	Shared Vision	Not being used	
Adaptive Planning	Practice	Scope Management	Overall Plan in place and reviewed periodically	
Requirements as Stories	Artefact	Work Breakdown	Stories are elaborated Just in Time by team including SME	
Progress Tracking / Velocity	Planning	Work Breakdown	Progress of work is measured and made highly visible.	
Retrospectives	Planning	Continuous Improvement	Retrospectives occur at least at the end of each iteration, and result in clear prioritised actions.	
Co-location	Practice	Close to Customer	Core team is co-located	
Requirements Gathering	Planning	Embracing Change	User Stories are used (instead of detailed Requirements documents) to capture the high-level requirements.	
Workshops (wisdom of the crowd)	Planning	Collaboration	Workshops are consistently used to achieve consensus	
Iteration Planning	Planning	Timeboxing	Iteration work/activities are planned and agreed	
Iterative Delivery	Practice	Collective Ownership	Team plans work to be delivered in iterative manner	

Frequent Small Releases	Artefact	Frequent Releases	Work is planned to provide deliverables at regular intervals	
Work Prioritisation	Planning	Close to Customer	Work is prioritised - MoSCoW	
Acceptance TDD	Practice	Quality Built-in	Work is done based on agreed acceptance criteria	
Architecture Design	Planning	Embracing Change	Not being used	
Agile reporting - Burn (Up/Down)	Artefact	Reporting	Not being used	
Agile reporting - Release Planning	Artefact	Planning	Not being used	
Rotation Model (Cross-Skilling)	Practice	Collective Ownership	Some Team members perform other roles	
Customer / SME is Available	Practice	Close to Customer	Customer/SME is always available, and they attend all the iteration rituals.	
Pair Delivery (Pair Programming)	Practice	Cross-skilling	Significant or complex work items are initiated in pairs to agree approach	
Test Driven Development	Practice	Quality Built-in	Not being used	
Continuous Integration	Practice	Frequent Releases	Continuous Integration builds solution on a regular basis	
Continuous Delivery	Practice	Frequent Releases	Not being used	
Automated Testing	Practice	Quality Built-in	Automated tests are written for majority test types	
Risk Management	Practice	Risk Management	Risk Register is not always visible to team and others	
Testing (including Unit / System / User Acceptance)	Practice	Timeboxing	Unit and System testing is performed within the iterations	

Refactoring	Practice	Quality Built-in	Not being used	
Spikes (timeboxed technical investigations)	Planning	Risk Management	Spikes are identified during work planning and used to uncover details of complex, high-risk or unestimated requirements	
Coding Standards	Artefact	Collective Ownership	Coding Standards defined and used	
Collective Code Ownership	Practice	Cross-skilling	All team members take responsibility for code changes, quality and maintenance	
Quality	Practice	Collective Ownership	The team is collectively responsible for defining and ensuring the quality of the deliverables.	
Team On-Boarding	People	Collaboration	Team Ways of Working are clearly defined and introduced to new team members.	
Business Value Estimates	Artefact	Close to Customer	Features have an associated Bus Value	
Risk / Issues / Blocker Management	Practice	Transparency	Risks/Issues are visualised on Team Wall	
Having Fun	People	Self-Organised	Regular fun (activities) in the team reduced stress and increased creativity.	
Iteration Management	People	Self-Organised	Team sees the Iteration Manager (Scrum Master) as a Servant-Leader	
Agile Governance	Planning	Reporting	Project Deliverables are	

				aligned to the Agile Deliverables (as opposed to the traditional milestones / funding)	
Self-Organizing Team	People		Self-Organised	The Project manager/ Iteration Manager (Scrum Master) is constantly pushing the team to become self-organising	

Based on user input, different types of Charts will be coming automatically.

Some sample Charts.

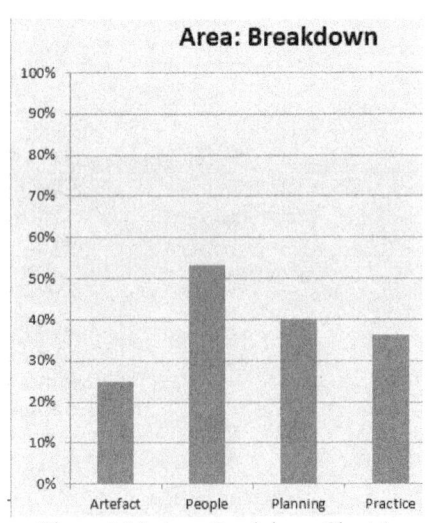

Figure 1.34: Area Breakdown Chart 1

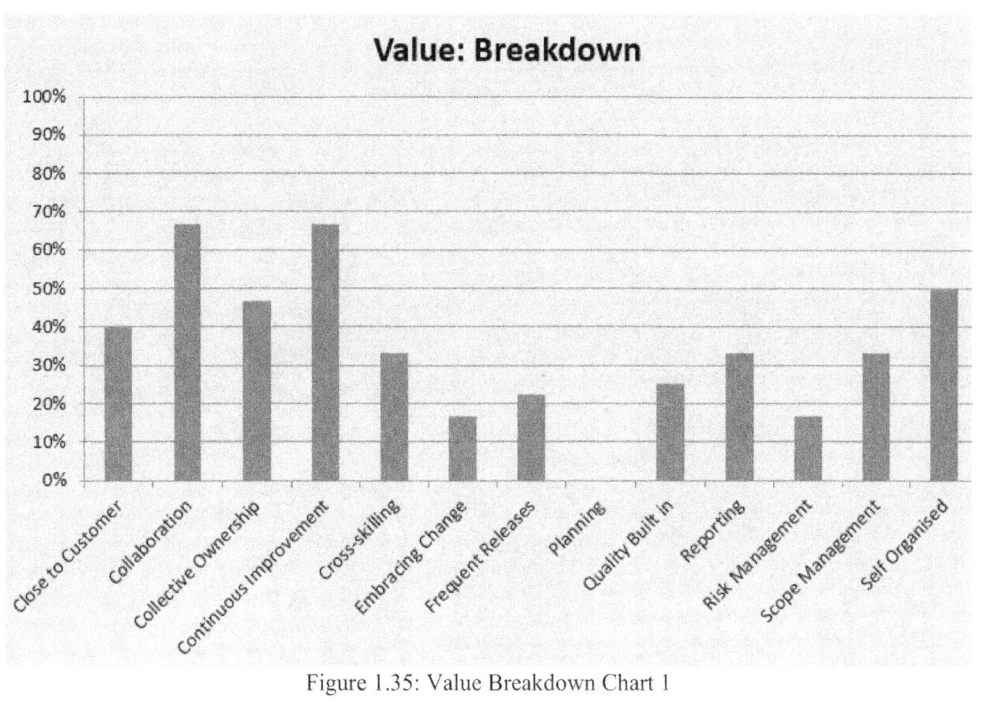

Figure 1.35: Value Breakdown Chart 1

Area: Breakdown

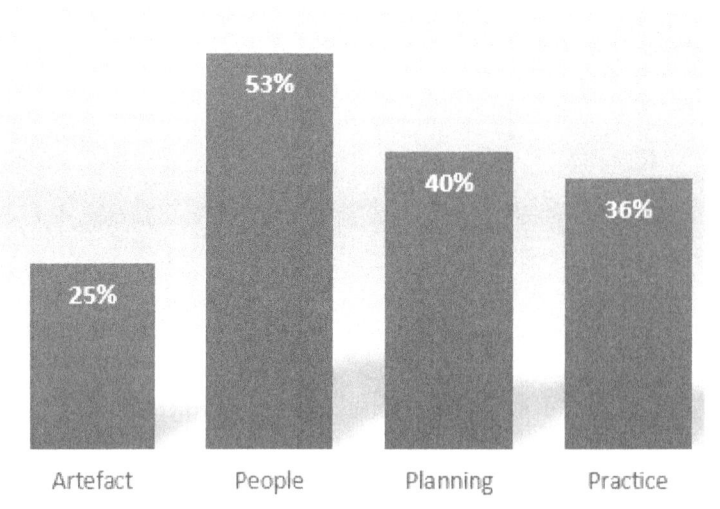

Artefact 25%	People 53%	Planning 40%	Practice 36%

Figure 1.36: Area Breakdown Chart 2

Value: Breakdown

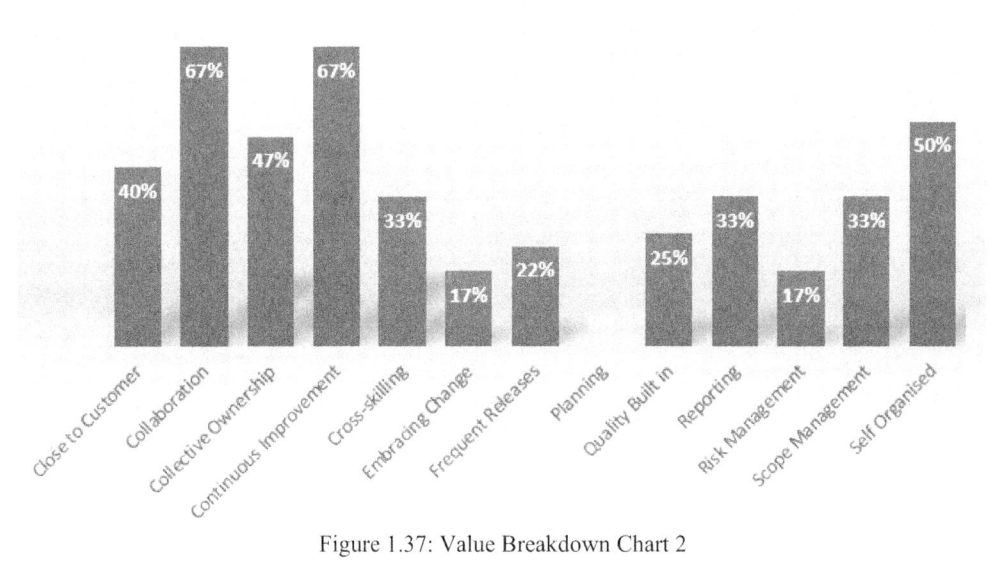

Category	Value
Close to Customer	40%
Collaboration	67%
Collective Ownership	47%
Continuous Improvement	67%
Cross-skilling	33%
Embracing Change	17%
Frequent Releases	22%
Planning	—
Quality Built in	25%
Reporting	33%
Risk Management	17%
Scope Management	33%
Self Organised	50%

Figure 1.37: Value Breakdown Chart 2

Area	Count	Rating	Max Rating	% Maturity
Artefact	8	6	24	25%
People	5	8	15	53%
Planning	10	12	30	40%
Practice	22	24	66	36%
Total	45	50	135	
Value				
Close to Custo	5	6	15	40%
Collaboration	3	6	9	67%
Collective Own	5	7	15	47%
Continuous Im	1	2	3	67%
Cross-skilling	2	2	6	33%
Embracing Cha	2	1	6	17%
Frequent Relea	3	2	9	22%
Planning	1	0	3	0%
Quality Built in	4	3	12	25%
Reporting	2	2	6	33%
Risk Managem	2	1	6	17%
Scope Manage	1	1	3	33%
Self Organised	4	6	12	50%
Shared Vision	1	0	3	0%
Sustainable Pa	1	1	3	33%
Timeboxing	3	4	9	44%
Transparency	3	3	9	33%
Work Breakdo	2	3	6	50%
Total	45	50	135	

Figure 1.38: Sample User input data

NOTES

NOTES

NOTES

NOTES

Chapter 2 - DevOps Introduction

DevOps is an approach based on the Lean and Agile principles in which business owners and the development, operations, and quality assurance departments collaborate to deliver IT solutions in a continuous manner that enables the business to seize market opportunities more quickly and reduce the time to include customer feedback.

- DevOps is a collaborative way of developing and deploying software.
- DevOps is a set of practices that provides rapid and reliable software delivery.
- DevOps is a movement that improves IT service delivery agility.
- DevOps is a set of practices that provides rapid, reliable software delivery.
- DevOps is a culture that promotes better working relationship within the company.
- DevOps is an environment that promotes cross practicality, shared business tasks and belief.

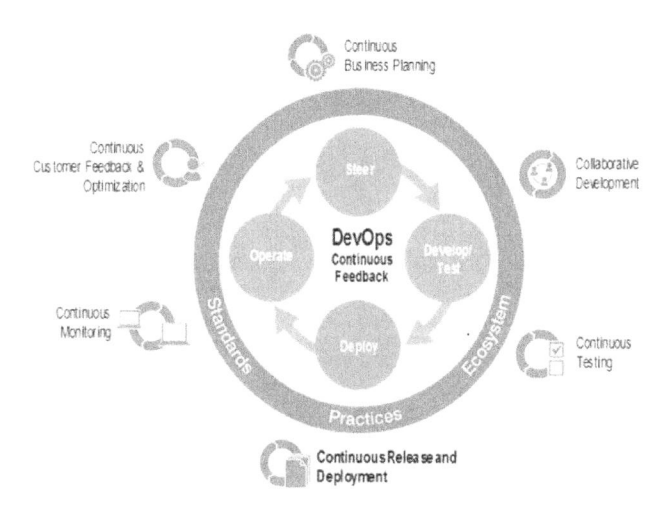

Figure 2.1 : DevOps in a nutshell

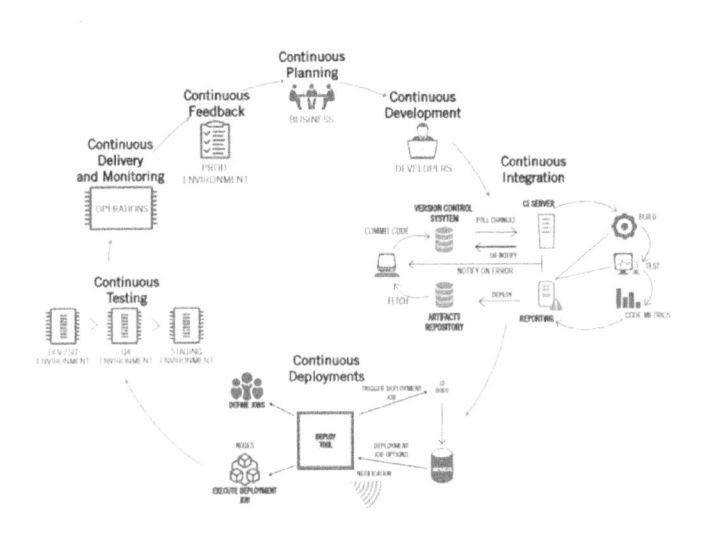

Figure 2.2 : DevOps in IT

Patrick Debois introduced DevOps in 2009; he is often known as *the father of DevOps*.

Need of DevOps: Developers want to deliver changes as soon as possible, but operations want reliability and stability.

Lee Thomson named it as a wall of confusion between the software developers and IT operations.

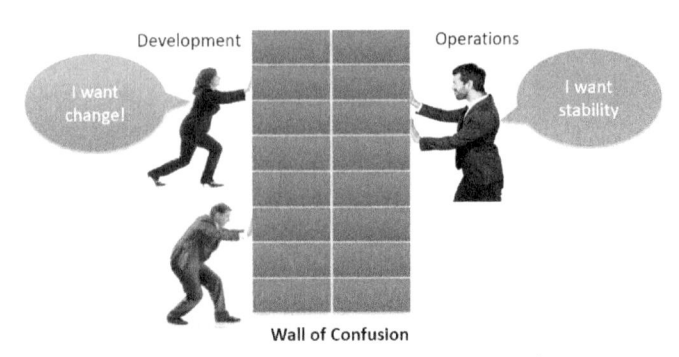

Figure 2.3 : Wall of Confusion silos

- The wall of confusion exists between the mind-set of both the teams and also within the tools they use.

- DevOps helps to break this wall of confusion, unifying the development to operations for better and for faster outcomes.

Wall of Confusion

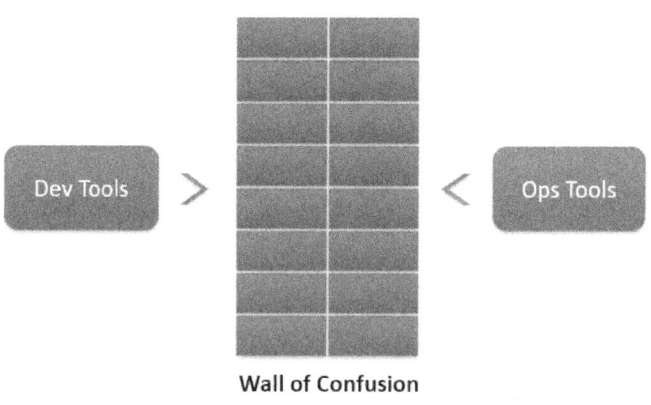

Figure 2.4 : Wall of Confusion

But DevOps is not:

a. Just limited to cloud
b. A role
c. Just confined to development
d. Just agile
e. Just for developers
f. Automation only

2.1. Principles of DevOps

- Business value for end user
- People Integration Metrics, KPI
- Ideas, Plans, Goals, Metrics, Complications, Tools
- Performance Metrics, Logs, Business goals Metrics,

- Continuous Delivery, Continuous Monitoring, Configuration Management
- Eliminate blame game, Open post-mortems, Feedback, Rewarding failures

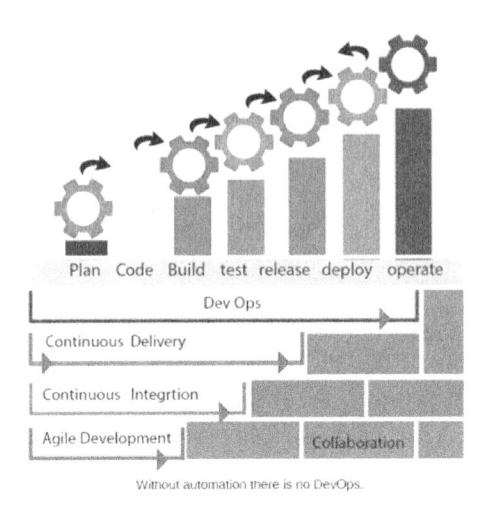

Figure 2.5 : DevOps Principles

2.2. Key Components of DevOps

- **Controlled Process (CP)**
- **Continuous Integration (CI)**
- **Continuous Deployment (CD)**
- **Continuous Testing (CT)**
- **Continuous Monitoring (CM)**
- Communication & Collaboration
- People – Communication & Collaboration
- Process – Source Control Check-ins, Code Review & Quality, Change Control, RCAs

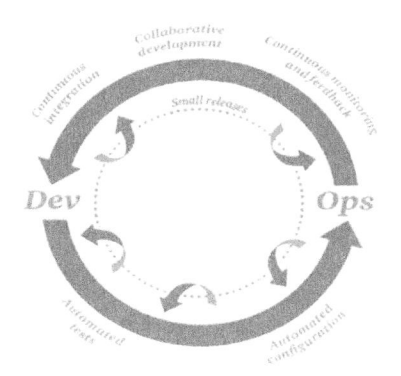

Figure 2.6 : DevOps – Key Components

2.3. DevOps Capabilities

- Automate Provisioning – Infrastructure as Code
- Automate Builds – Continuous Integration
- Automate Deployments – Defined Deployment Pipeline and
- Continuous Deployments with appropriate configurations for the environments
- Automate Testing – Continuous Testing, Automated tests after each deployment
- Automate Monitoring – Proper monitors in place sending alerts
- Automate Metrics – Performance Metrics, Logs

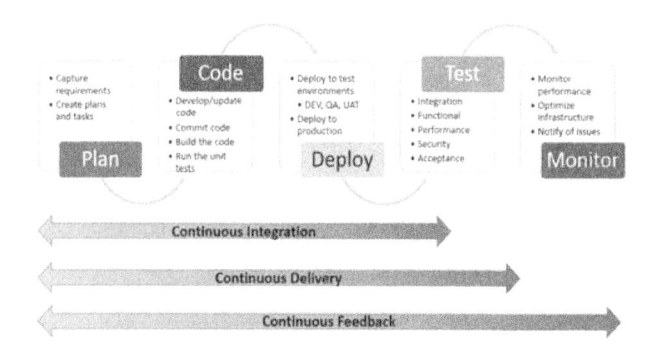

Figure 2.7 : DevOps Capabilities

- **Six DevOps Capabilities**

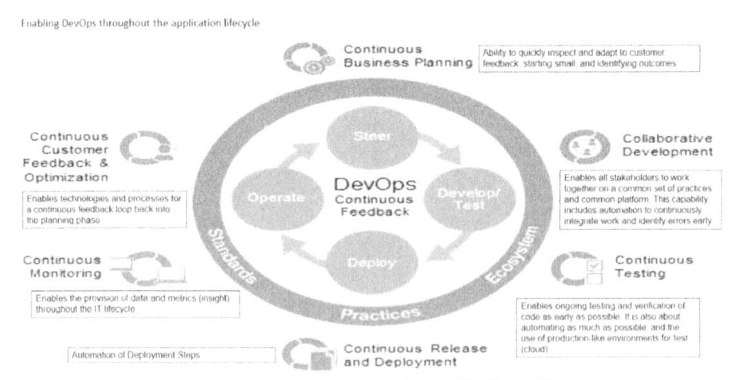

Figure 2.8 : DevOps – Six Capabilities

2.4. DevOps Purpose & Objectives

DevOps combines the best of all teams providing
- Minimizes rollbacks
- Reduces Deployment related downtime
- Increases Virtualize Environments utilization
- Develops and verifies against production-like systems
- Increases Quality – Automated testing, Reduce cost/time to test
- Reduces Defect cycle time – Increase the ability to reproduce and fix defects
- Reduces cost/time to deliver – Deploy often & faster with repeatable, reliable process

2.5. DevOps Triggering Points

- Need to reduce IT costs
- Need to improve the end customer experience
- The increasing need to develop or deploy cloud based applications
- A greater need for simultaneous deployment across different platforms
- The need for greater collaboration between development and operations terms
- An increasingly complex IT infrastructure that is part physical, part virtualized, and part cloud
- Pressures from business to release applications more quickly to meet customer demand or enter new markets

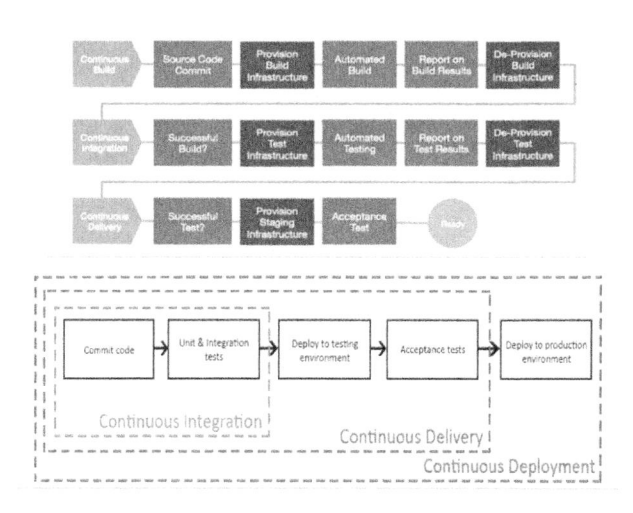

Figure 2.9 : What drives the needs of DevOps

2.6. DevOps and People, Process and Technology

- DevOps is a culture which promotes collaboration between Development and Operations Team to deploy code to production faster in an automated and repeatable way. The word 'DevOps' is a combination of two words *development* and *operations*.
- A way of working – a combination of: *People, Process & Tools*
- DevOps is a *philosophy* of the *efficient development, deployment and operation*, of the highest quality software possible.
- An alignment of development and IT operations with better communication and collaboration.
- About *eliminating inefficiencies & bottlenecks* in the software delivery lifecycle.
- DevOps is an *approach based on Lean and Agile principles* in which business owners and the development, operations, quality assurance departments collaborate to deliver software in a continuous manner that enables the business to more quickly seize market opportunities and *reduce the time to include customer feedback*.

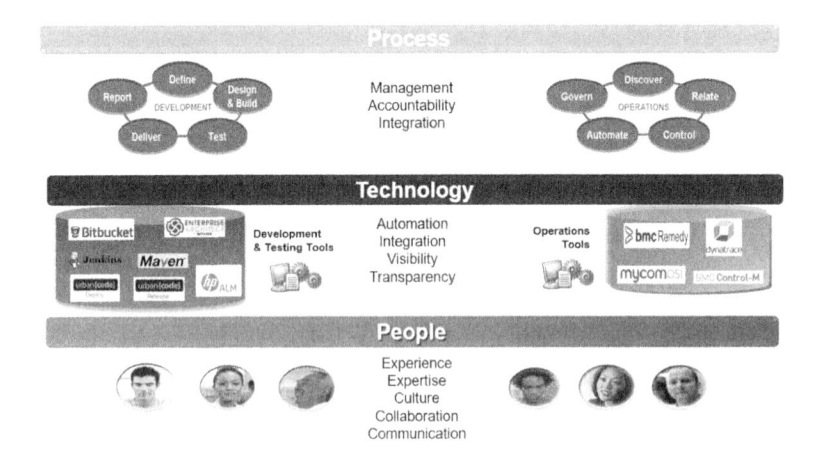

Figure 2.10 : DevOps – People, Process and Technology

DevOps is a culture that promotes the following:

- People first, then Process and then Technology (PPT)
- Better working relationship within the company
- Continual experimentation, which requires taking risks and learning from success and failure
- Understanding that the repetition and practice are the prerequisites to mastery

2.7. DevOps "Why" & "What"

a. What's in it for Individuals

- Get involved in the end to end process of developing, testing & delivering the business features to clients.
- Monitoring how these features are performing.
- Accept more responsibility in turn getting credit for the value they bring to clients.
- Have better understanding of the role, their work & code play for the product & business.
- Rich technical learning experience.
- Learn industry transforming technologies, product and enhance their technical abilities, making them competitive.

b. **Why should Customer adopt DevOps**

- DevOps was the Mantra for success yesterday/ it is the mantra for survival today.
- You would be obsolete even if you think you would look at it in six months.
- The business cannot compete in the market if it cannot deliver faster in a continuous way on day to day basis.
- Customer is expecting immediate resolution of his/her feedback – immediate is NOW.
- Every Business is linked in some way with CAMS and the end customer expectations are 'everything now'.

2.8. DevOps – Key Takeaways

The needs for DevOps must be driven for Business.

- We covered this still anyway here we go.
- DevOps is not Automation but Automation is the stepping stone in the DevOps adoption.
- DevOps is a combination of culture, processes, and tools.
- Automation, if not continuous will not help.
- Automation at every stage when integrated to the next stage resulting into continuous delivery, that is DevOps!

DevOps is not:

- Just limited to cloud
- A role
- Just confined to development
- Just agile
- Just for developers
- Automation only

DevOps is much more than agile:

- DevOps is complementary to agile
- Agile focuses on the software development process
- DevOps extends and completes the continuous integration and release process

DevOps – Technical Benefits
- Continuous software delivery
- Less complexity
- Faster issue resolutions

DevOps – Business Benefits
- Faster delivery of features
- More stable operating environment
- Improved communication & collaboration
- More time to innovate

DevOps – Cultural Benefits
- Happier, more productive teams
- Higher employee engagement
- Greater professional development opportunities
- Integrated process and teams

2.9. DevOps – Impediments

It doesn't matter whether you are in Cloud, Enterprise or Mobile.
For each of *Stable Software Delivery*, *On-Time* is the key to business success.

Key Challenges for Implementing DevOps Strategy
- **Production downtime**: to lack of improper deployment instructions / checklist.
- **No proper SCM management**: Discrepancies in managing configurations, No Code Baseline management.
- Broken Build, Deployment, Continuous Integration, Continuous Testing framework → SaaS Managed Apps.
- **Hacking**: Fixing directly in PROD (instead of a proper hotfix process) and forgets to check-in into source control.
- No Environment Strategy and Principles. Each Vendor/Provider has its own concept/rule to manage Environment / process.
- **Deployments are a blocker**: Upgrade risk due to manual management of multiple application configuration and versions, Dependency on specific deployment SME.

Key Issues Blocking Software Delivery?
- No shared ownership – Lack of feedback and proper metric leads
- Slow deployments – Costly error prone manual process and efforts
- Building and maintaining servers – Time consuming and unproductive
- No environment management - Differences in development and production environments

Key obstacles in implementing DevOps in an organization?
- Tools don't work well together.
- It's unknown, not testified, must be too expensive!!

97

- I can't get my management to buy into new processes.
- The value of DevOps isn't understood outside my group.
- DevOps is too new and I don't have the support, I need to be successful.
- There is no common management structure between development and operations.
- Its someone's action or dream or an organization initiative, I would go as per traditional norms.

3.0. DevOps – Value Stream Example

Illustrated with an example view of **Value realization**, once DevOps solution is implemented covering all aspects *People, Process, Application, Tools, Methods* and so on.

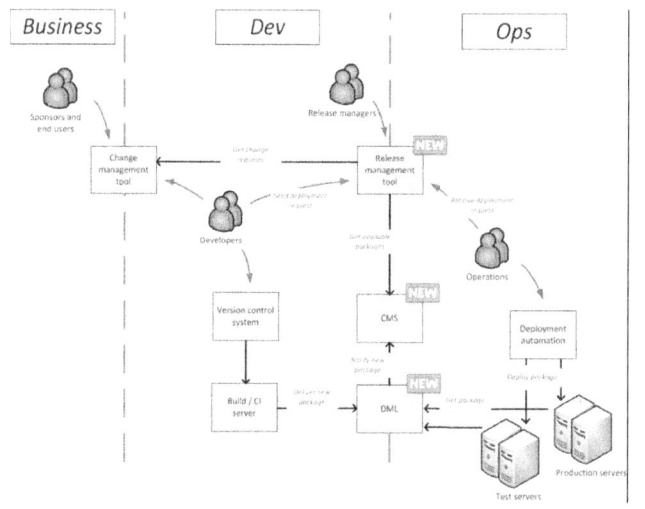

Figure 2.11 : DevOps Framework – Delivery Value Realization (Sample)

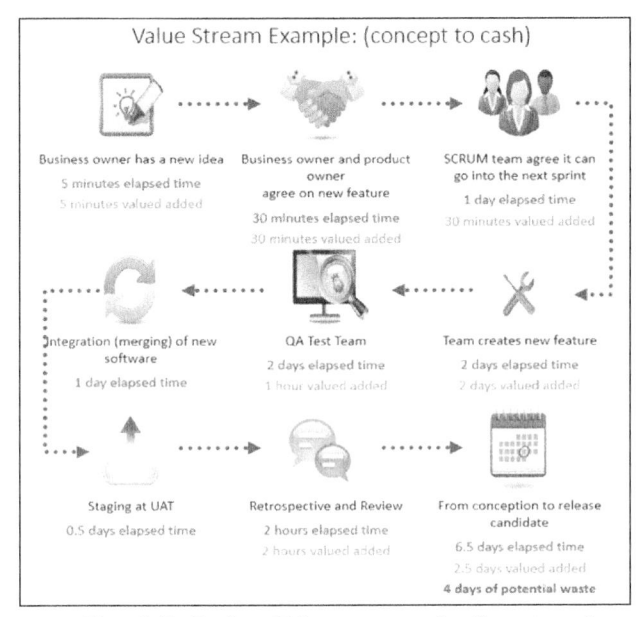

Figure 2.12 : DevOps – Value stream example – Concept to cash

3.1. DevOps Framework – Definitions and Overview

Why DevOps

Business Benefits

- Faster delivery of features
- More stable operating environment
- Improved communication & collaboration
- More time to innovate

Technical Benefits
- Continuous software delivery
- Less complexity
- Faster issue resolutions

Cultural Benefits
- Happier, more productive teams
- Higher employee engagement
- Greater professional development opportunities
- Integrated process and teams

- Before DevOps, the development and operation team worked in complete isolation.
- Testing and Deployment were isolated activities done after design-build. Hence, they consumed more time than actual build cycles.
- Without using DevOps, team members are spending a *large amount of their time in testing, and deploying* instead of building the project.
- Manual code deployment leads to *human errors* in production.
- Coding & operation teams have their separate timelines and are not in *sync* causing further delays.
- There is a demand to increase *the rate of software delivery* by business stakeholders.

As per Forrester Consulting Study, Only 17% of teams can use delivery software fast enough. This proves the PAIN POINT.

3.2. DevOps follows CALMS model

C ulture	• Hearts and minds • Embrace change
A utomation	• CI / CD • Infrastructure as code
L ean	• Focus on production value for the end-user • Small batch sizes
M easurement	• Measure everything • Show the improvement
S haring	• Open information sharing • Collaboration

3.3. DevOps – Work Practices vs Phase

- DevOps takes and end-to-end approach of software delivery.
- Previous practices (example: Agile) addressed only a subset of value chain.

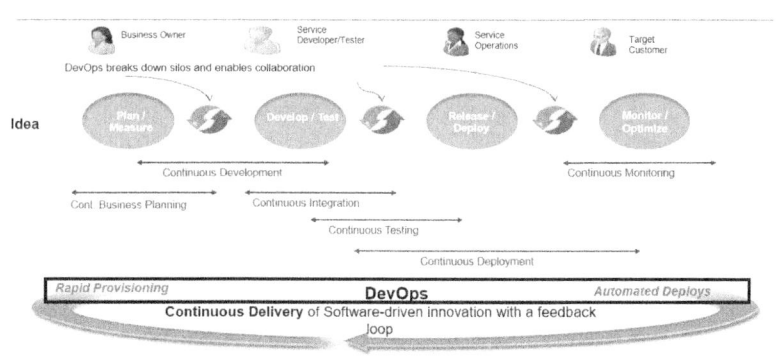

Figure 2.13 : DevOps "Capability Framework Model"

3.4. DevOps – Work Products

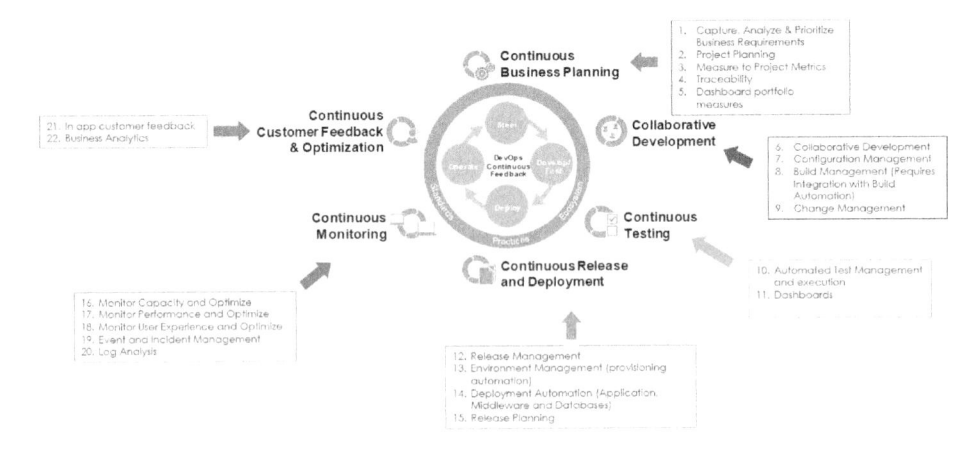

Figure 2.14 : 6C's and 22 Principles of DevOps

3.5. DevOps Practice - Continuous Business Planning

A. **Key opportunities or pain which can be addressed by this practice**
   - Requirement Traceability from source to production deployment.
   - Phase wise release planning in multiple sprints .
   - Adoption to design thinking
   - Plan to adopt the Delivery Pipeline in the IBM Blue mix Continuous Delivery.
   - Teams needs to be guided on culture, best DevOps practices, tools, self-guided or hands-on training—even sample code and architectures for developers.
   - Transform the team from slow, siloed teams to a self-managing, solution-oriented, bottleneck-free, go-fast team.
   - Extending lean principles across the entire software supply chain.
   - Operations should measure not only the increase in speed of releases but also the impact of the releases on cost and on customer value.

B. **Primary set of tools which can be used to effectively implement this Practice**
   - JIRA
   - RTVM
   - Muller, CA Agile
   - Tool Chain
   - IBM Rational Team Concert

C. **Key Business & IT benefits which can be driven from this practice**
   - Acceptance Criteria can be defined as business outcome rather than just IT test cases execution

- Change traceability from requirements to production
- Ensuring Robust integrated solutions to the overall delivery at each phase of application development and its operations.
- Using Agile methodology, development teams are able to shrink development cycles dramatically and increase application quality.

3.6. DevOps Practice - Collaborative Development

A. Key Opportunities or Pain which can be addressed by this practice
- By integrating the system more frequently, integration issues are identified earlier, when they are easier to fix, and the overall integration effort is reduced.
- Change sets from all developers are integrated in a team workspace, and then built and unit tested frequently. This should happen at least daily, but ideally it happens any time a new change set is available.
- Integrate and automate build, deploy, testing, and promotion to obtain quick resolutions to the issues identified.
- Team to be collaborated via communication tools for each set of changes on build.
- Developers must develop the discipline and skills to organize their work into small, cohesive change sets.

B. Primary set of Tools which can be used to effectively implement this Practice
- RTVM
- GIT HUB
- HP –UFT
- ALM
- IBM Box
- HipChat
- Confluence
- BitBucket
- IBM Connections
- IBM Verse
- Slack
- Jenkins
- IBM Urban Code Build
- IBM Rational Collaborative Lifecycle Management (CLM)

C. Key Business & IT benefits which can be driven from this Practice
- The result is a higher quality product and more predictable delivery schedules.
- Changes are made to a configuration that is known to be good and tested before the new code is available.
- Improved error detection.
- Integrate and test the system on every change to minimize the time between injecting a defect and correcting it.

- By integrating continuously throughout the project, continuous build happens for each set of changes, thereby mitigating integration surprises at the end of the lifecycle.

3.7. DevOps Practice - Continuous Testing

A. **Key Opportunities or Pain which can be addressed by this practice**
   - Requirement traceability for each test cases.
   - Regression suite pack automation and auto execution after each build being system tested.
   - Cognitive approach to do predictive analysis on defects.
   - Defect management - Daily checkpoints on defects fixes with all integration interfaces stakeholders.
   - Cognitive analytics to produce the periodical frequent dashboard

B. **Primary set of Tools which can be used to effectively implement this Practice**
   - RTVM
   - Muller, CA Agile
   - Selenium
   - ALM, Win runner,
   - Tool chain
   - JUnit
   - Cognitive – Watson explorer
   - Rational Test Virtualization Server
   - IBM Worklight Quality Assurance

C. **Key Business & IT benefits which can be driven from this practice**
   - Acceptance Criteria can be defined as business outcome after each build being executed for testing.
   - Staged builds will provide a useful means to organize testing to get the right balance between coverage and speed.
   - Predictive analysis dashboard with current health of project and future prediction can alarm client at every stage on the state of the product delivery.
   - Using DevOps insights, one can explore project's defects data by viewing the dashboards in the data category.

3.8. DevOps Practice - Continuous Deployments

A. **Key Opportunities or Pain which can be addressed by this practice**
   - Team can be more productive, less stressed, and more focused on feature delivery rather than dealing with big, unknown potential changes.

- If every change is releasable, it has to be entirely self-contained. That includes things like user documentation, operations runbooks, and information about exactly what changed and how for audits and traceability.
- Deliver through an automated pipeline.
- Automate not only builds and code deployments, but even the process of constructing new development, test, and production environments.
- Implement blue-green deployments.
- Pain area:
    - Difficult to automate the process of constructing new developments as the most of the applications hosted on premise environment using different technologies difficult to bring all together in automated way . Way forward would be to use Blue mix and find the scope of building API and connect the process with automation scripts.

B. **Primary set of tools which can be used to effectively implement this practice**
- RTVM
- Muller, CA Agile
- GIT HUB
- Tool chain
- ANT
- Bamboo
- Release management tools – SNOW, Remedy
- Docker
- IBM Urban code Deploy

C. **Key Business & IT benefits which can be driven from this Practice**
- Acceptance Criteria can be defined as business outcome after each build being executed for Testing.
- Staged builds will provide a useful means to organize testing to get the right balance between coverage and speed.
- The key to building a good delivery pipeline is to automate nearly everything in the development process.
- Aim for zero downtime.

3.9. DevOps Practice - Continuous Monitoring

A. **Key Opportunities or Pain which can be addressed by this practice**
- Automated Monitoring tools to measure application response time every few minutes from around the globe.
- Most often, the dependencies that one application has on other components or services is not tracked regularly.
- Integrate automated monitoring with rich notification tooling.
- Access the efficiency of automated monitoring tools.
- Monitoring and analytics services on Bluemix.
- Pain area:

- o Automated monitoring leads to some form of failure or performance degradation due to the complexity of the applications.
- Solution: Use collaboration tools, such as Slack or Google Hangouts, to collectively solve problems with the help of SME's on various service areas involved.

B. **Primary set of tools which can be used to effectively implement this practice**
  - ServiceNow, Remedy
  - PagerDuty, Nettool (Netpin notification)
  - Slack, Google hangout
  - Control M, CRON jobs
  - IBM Bluemix Availability monitoring
  - IBM Monitoring and Analytics
  - NewRelic, Pingdom,
  - Datadog, Uptime, Sensu
  - IBM Alert Notification
  - Dynatrace
  - AppDynamics
  - Splunk, Sumologic

C. **Key Business & IT benefits which can be driven from this Practice**
  - Quick identification of the root cause of an issue, through the use of line-of-code diagnostics.
  - Faster time to resolve application's issue by using embedded analytics to search log and metric data.
  - Good automated monitoring is being able to recognize trends that lead to a problem.
  - Instant visibility and transparency into the application's performance and health without the need to learn or deploy other tools.
  - Reduced maintenance costs, as the application keeps running with minimal effort.

4.0. DevOps Practice - Continuous Customer Feedback and Optimization

A. **Key Opportunities or Pain which can be addressed by this practice**
  - The most important metric to track in the cloud is time to recovery for any defect/down time.
  - In today's global marketplace, websites are expected to be always available.
  - To meet the SLA goal, the Garage Method team took these actions:
    - o Implement a continuous delivery process by using IBM Blue mix Continuous Delivery.
    - o Implement a *Deploy to Test* stage.
    - o Implement blue-green deployment.
    - o Deploy the production website to multiple Blue mix data centers.
  - Write and maintain runbooks to troubleshoot operational issues.
  - Surface SLA reports that clearly show daily, weekly, and monthly outage data.

B. **Primary set of tools which can be used to effectively implement this practice**
  - Runbook Automation
  - Tool Chains

- Delivery Pipeline
- IBM Tea leaf
- IBM Smart Cloud Analytics—Log Analysis

C. **Key business & IT benefits which can be driven from this practice**
   - Continuously gain new insights from the customers' interaction about the application and the metrics collected to drive business decisions.
   - Shift operational practices to the front of the development cycle to improve reliability.
   - DevOps is the leading way to develop and deliver competitive applications and solutions to the market.
   - Deliver a differentiated and engaging customer experience that builds customer loyalty and increases market share by continuously obtaining and responding to customer feedback.
   - Respond to the market faster and ensure an outstanding customer experience.
   - DevOps capabilities will improve productivity through accelerated customer feedback cycles, unified measurements and collaboration across an enterprise, and reduced overhead, duplication, and rework.

5.0. DevOps Capabilities – Framework Model & Principles

5.1. DevOps "Capability Framework Model"

- DevOps takes an end-to-end approach of software delivery
- Previous practices (example: Agile) addressed only a subset of value chain

Goal: Get ideas into market/production fast, get people use it, get feedback

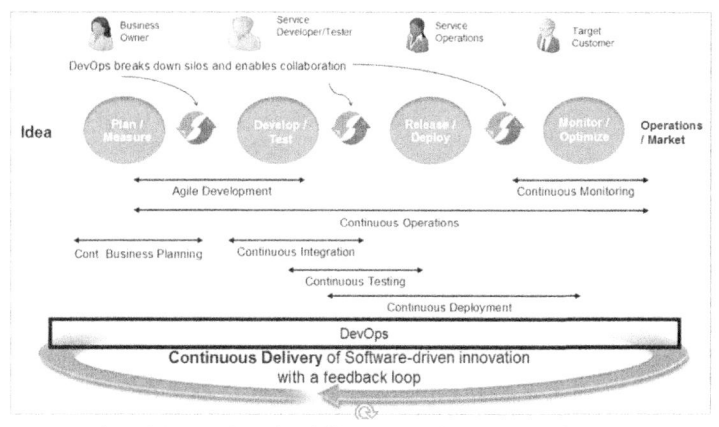

Figure 2.15 : DevOps "Capability Framework Model" overview

Figure 2.16 : DevOps "Capability Framework Model" illustration

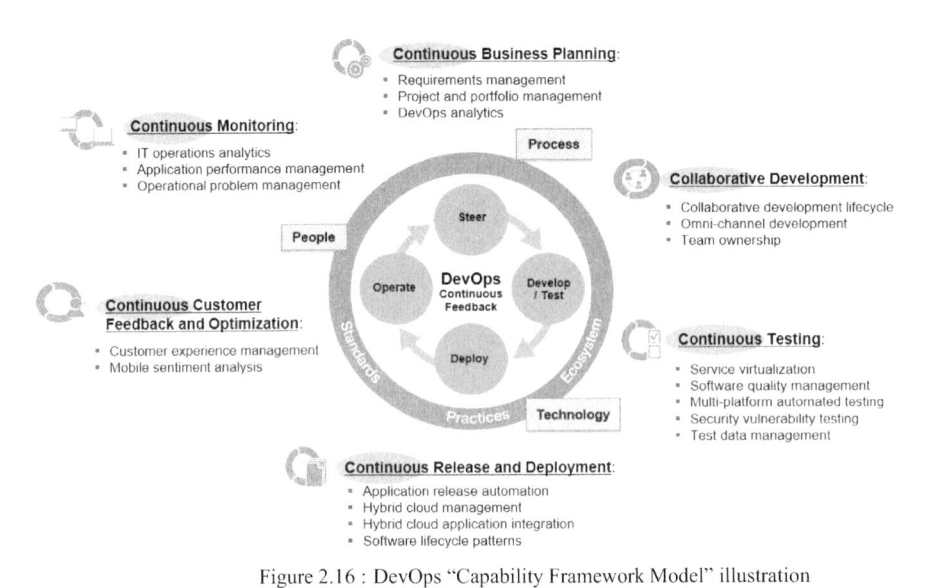

5.2. DevOps "Capability Framework Principles"

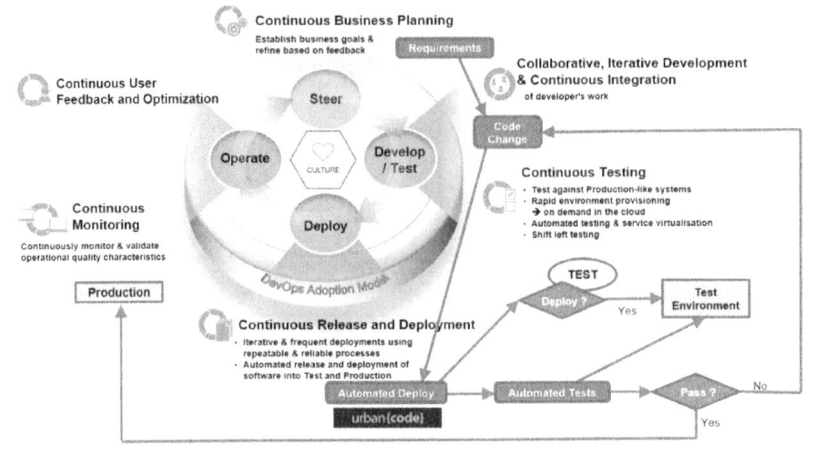

Figure 2.17 : DevOps "Capability Framework Principles"

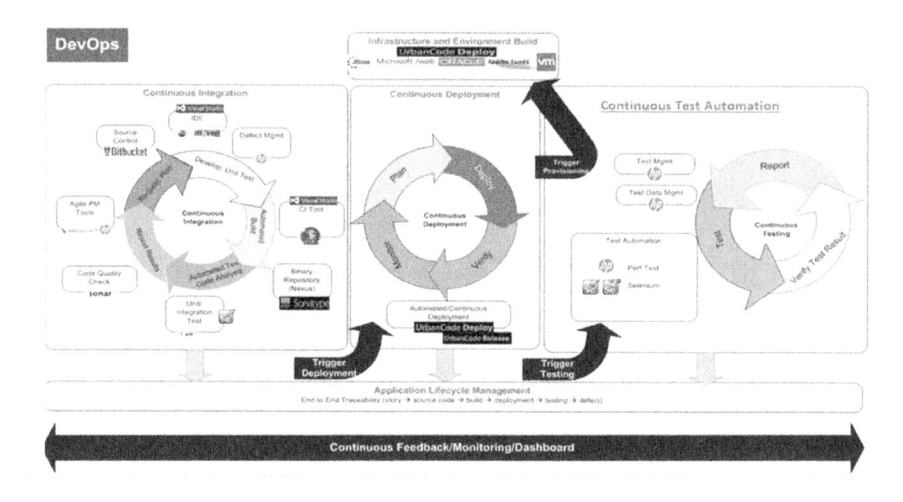

Figure 2.18 : DevOps "Capability Framework Principles" overview

5.3 DevOps "Operating Model" Framework

Please find it enclosed below.

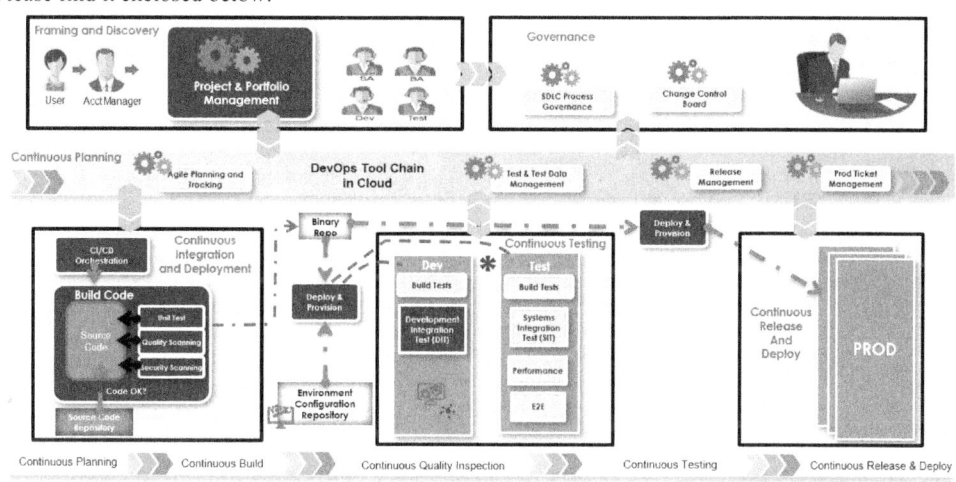

Figure 2.19: DevOps "Operating Model" Framework overview

Please tailor it as applicable based on your customer requirement.

5.4 DevOps "Tools" with "SDLC Phases" - Demo

Picture illustrates with SDLC project delivery model, using *different tools* to integrate per Application/Product component to realize DevOps delivery solution model.

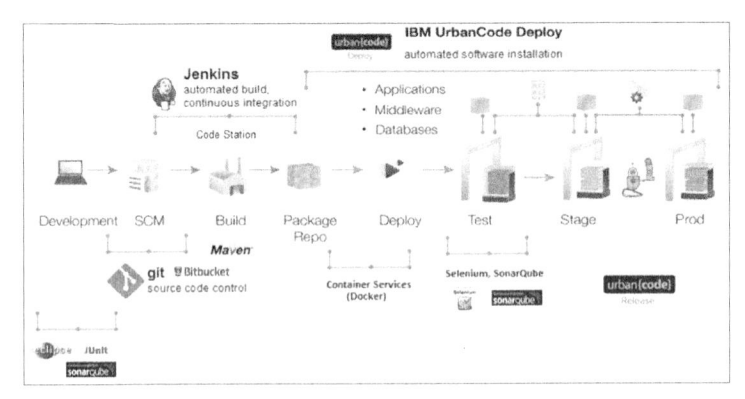

Figure 2.20 : DevOps "Tools" with "SDLC Phases" – Sample

5.5 DevOps "Tooling Framework" – VALUE Chain DEMO

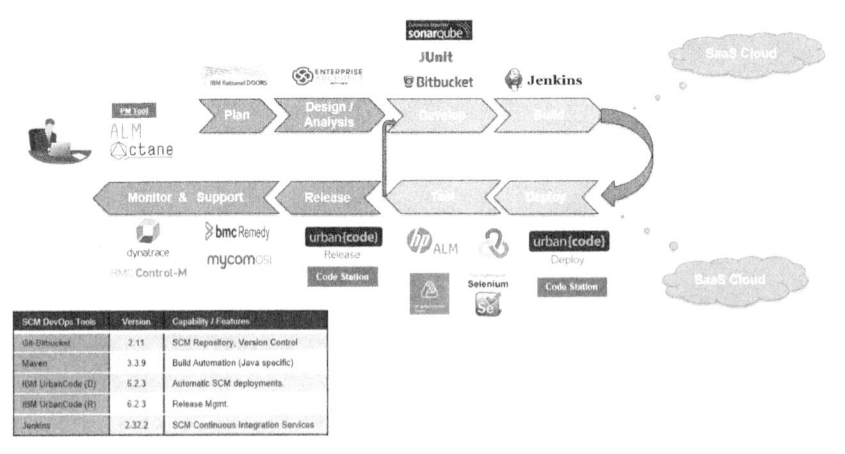

Figure 2.21 : DevOps "Tooling Framework" – Value Chain Example

5.6 SDLC / ALM Framework- Phase & Tool Example - DEMO

The following picture illustrates with the SDLC/ALM phases, with its tools usage for DevOps framework (CI, CD) to manage expected outcomes.
Within SDLC/ALM, we also illustrate QA models using traditional, Agile and DevOps, on how "*QA benefits with built-in QC controls*" for DevOps.

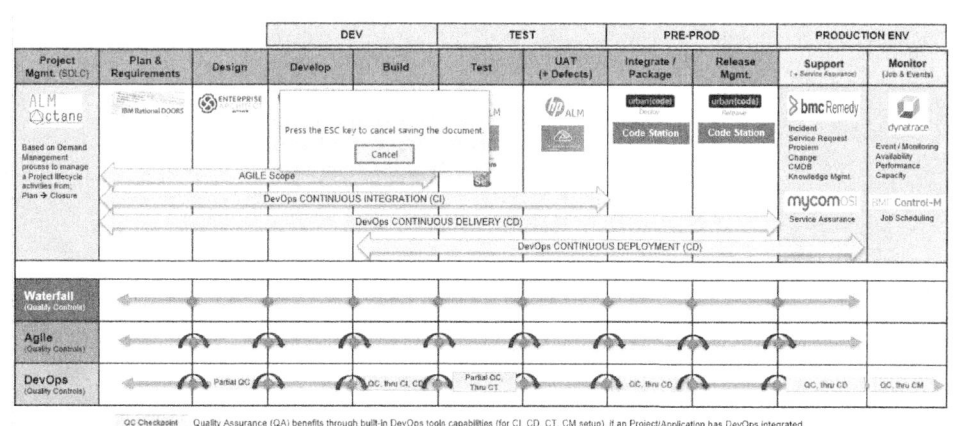

Figure 2.22: SDLC / ALM Framework – Phase & Tool Example

5.7 DevOps "Continuous Business Planning"

A simplified view across the development and delivery lifecycles
maximize business outcomes and value through an open collaborative, standards-based platform and strong governance framework.

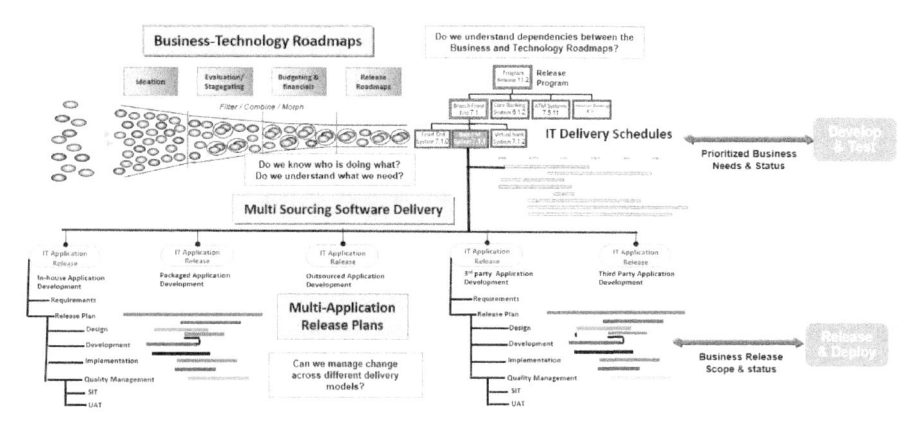

Figure 2.23: DevOps "Continuous Business Planning"

5.8 DevOps "Continuous Integration & Continuous Testing"

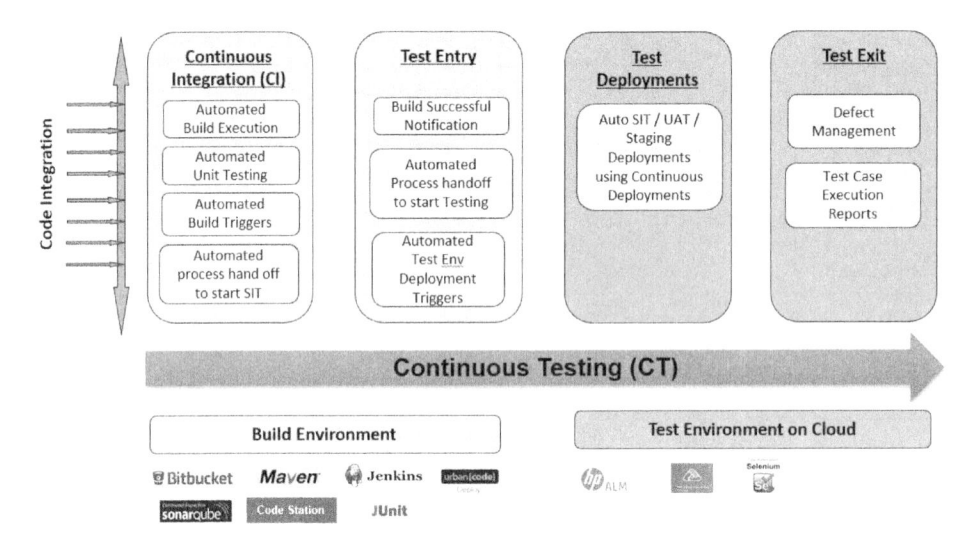

Figure 2.24: DevOps "Continuous Integration & Continuous Testing" overview

5.9 DevOps "Continuous Deployment & Release Management"

It provides a continuous delivery pipeline which automate deployments to test on production like environments. It reduces the amount of manual labor, resource wait-time, and rework by means of push-button deployments that allow higher frequency of releases, reduced errors, and end-to-end transparency for compliance.

The continuous release and deployment practice within DevOps addresses existing problems in traditional software development, such as:
- Teams using different tools across the software development lifecycle
- Processes that do not scale to the complexity of applications
- Conflicts between development and operations

Continuous deployment is closely related to continuous integration and refers to the release into production of software that passes the automated tests.

Continuous Deploy
- Promoting multi-tiered SCM code through to production
- Versioning deployment artifacts
- Managing incremental deployment changes
- Deployments to middleware environments
- Database change deployments
- Deployment snapshots
- Rollbacks

Continuous release
- Manage environment changes in release events
- Track infrastructure and application changes through a release
- Orchestrate releases of inter-dependent applications
- Facilitate release collaborations

And it offers following benefits

- Speed time to market
- Stable and predictable releases
- Increased visibility
- Fewer outages & efficient rollbacks if required
- Release better software more often

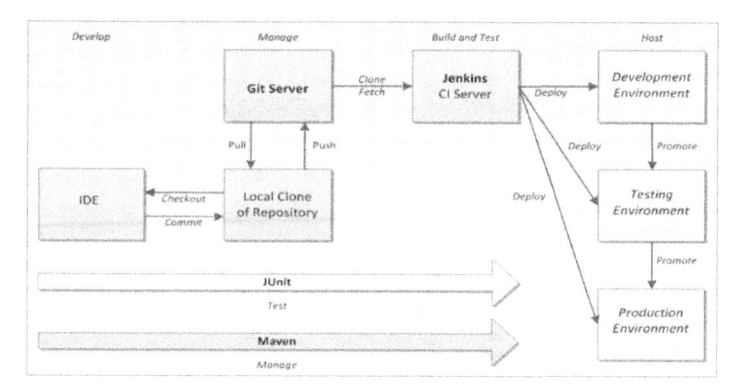

Figure 2.25: DevOps "Continuous Deployment & Release Management" overview

5.10 DevOps "Continuous Release Management"

What's a Release?
Release is a workable software product labeled or named with some number or name.
It is produced to deliver specific requirements. It's normally incremental and produced out of SDLC phases.

What's a Deployment?
The activity responsible for movement of approved releases of hardware, software, documentation, processes etc. to any environments.

Release & Deployment Activities
1. Release planning (Release Calendar)
2. Prepare for build, test and deployment
3. Build and verify
4. Testing
5. Plan and prepare for production deployment
6. Perform production deployment

7. Verify production deployment
8. Early life cycle support
9. Review and close release

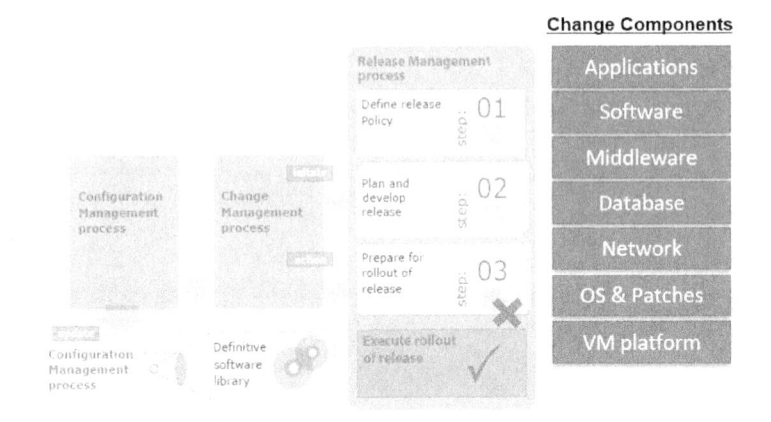

Figure 2.26: DevOps "Continuous Release Management" overview

5.11 DevOps "Continuous Release & Deployment Automation"

- **IBM UrbanCode** deploy provides an automation deployment framework that reduces deployment errors and improves efficiency, correctness, and traceability.
- **IBM UrbanCode** release orchestrates the *major release* ensuring multiple applications are successfully released.

Key Benefits:
- **Reduce errors:** Automated software release and deployment.
- **Improve productivity**: Push-button deployments for developer and operations.
- **Faster time-to-market:** Automated release and deployment with built-in best practices provides.
- **Compliance and auditability:** Enforced security and traceability.

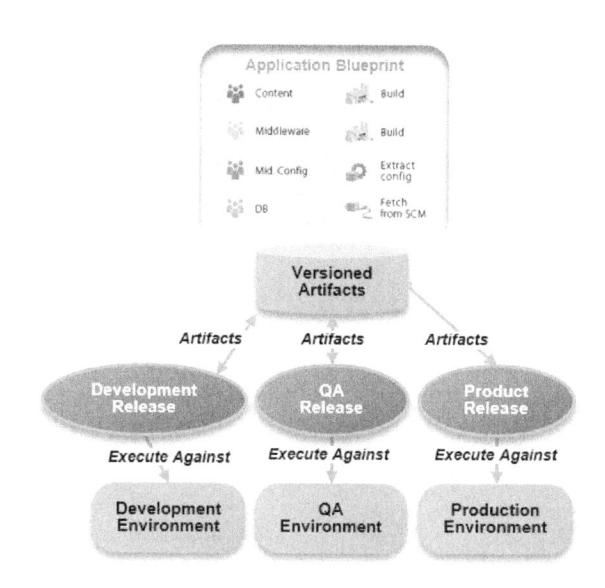

Figure 2.27: DevOps "Continuous Release & Deployment Automation" overview

5.12 DevOps "Capabilities" using "Quality Assurance"

The key automated *QA controls* within *DevOps Framework* can be focused through its *DevOps Tools* within its Continuous Delivery, Continuous Integration phase activities, as illustrated as follows:

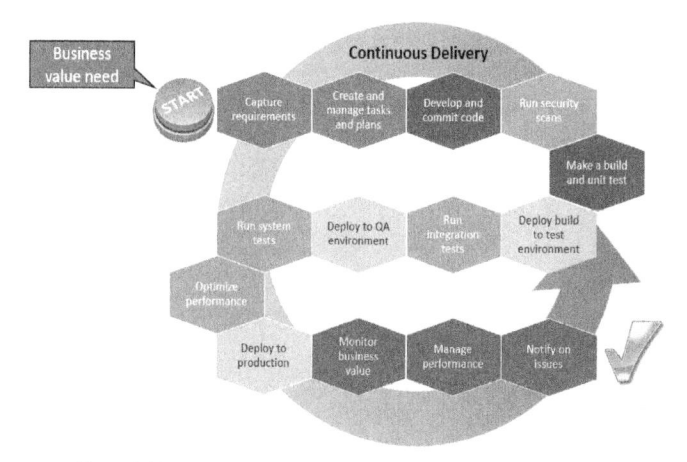

Figure 2.28: DevOps "Capabilities" using "Quality Assurance" overview

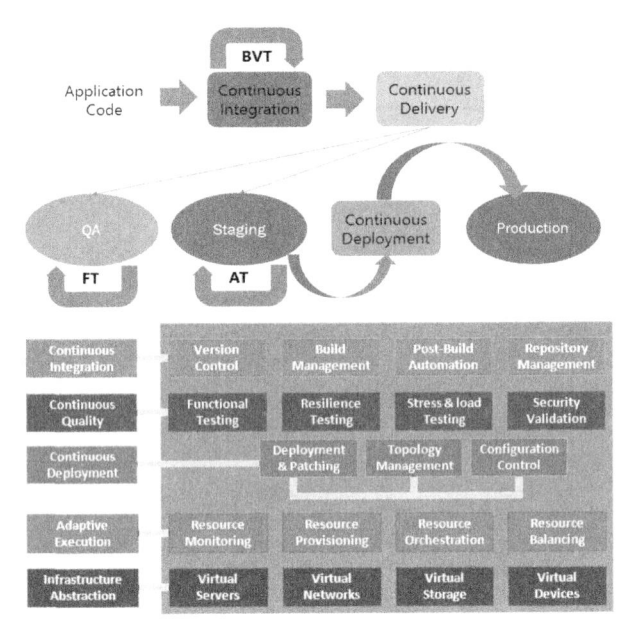

Figure 2.29: DevOps "Capabilities" using "Quality Assurance" process

5.13 DevOps "Continuous Delivery" with in-built "Quality Assurance"

In a matured DevOps situation (Level-5), we can foresee QA built-in within each of DevOps focus phases/stages, thus ensuring quality checkpoint and integral to its next iterative phase or dependent activity.
Following screenshot, illustrates with the DevOps framework listing its phases of a project SDLC / application ALM, with its relation possible automation controls defined as per DevOps QA policy / principles.

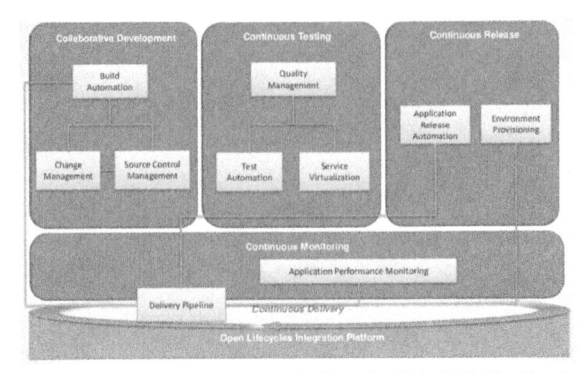

Figure 2.30: DevOps "Continuous Delivery" with in-built "Quality Assurance"

115

Continuous delivery flow

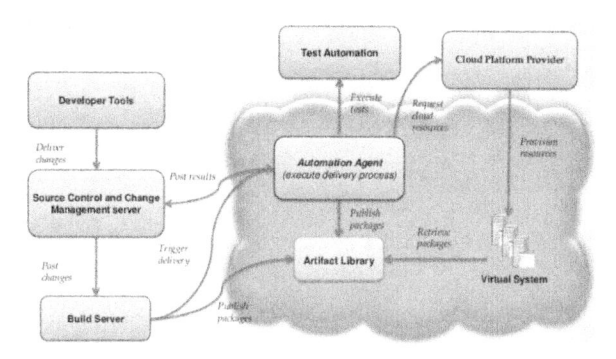

Figure 2.31: DevOps "Continuous Delivery" flow

5.14 DevOps "Capabilities" with in-built "Quality Assurance"

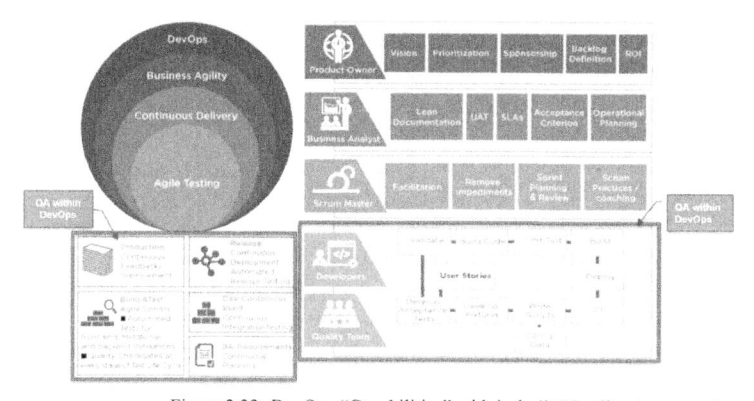

Figure 2.32: DevOps "Capabilities" with in-built "Quality Assurance"

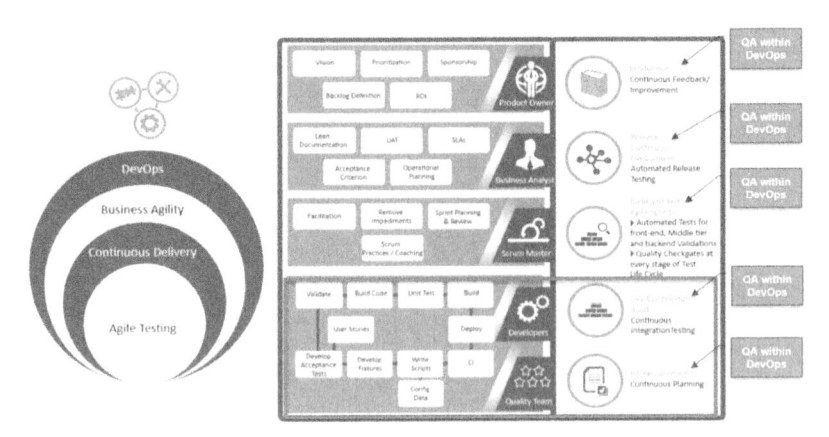

Figure 2.33: DevOps "Capabilities" with in-built "Quality Assurance" process overview

5.15. DevOps for Testing – Within SDLC Framework

5.15.1 SDLC (Testing Phase): Testing Framework for Agile Projects, using DevOps Methods

E2E Testing, supported by DevOps accelerators & Continuous Improvements & Integrations.

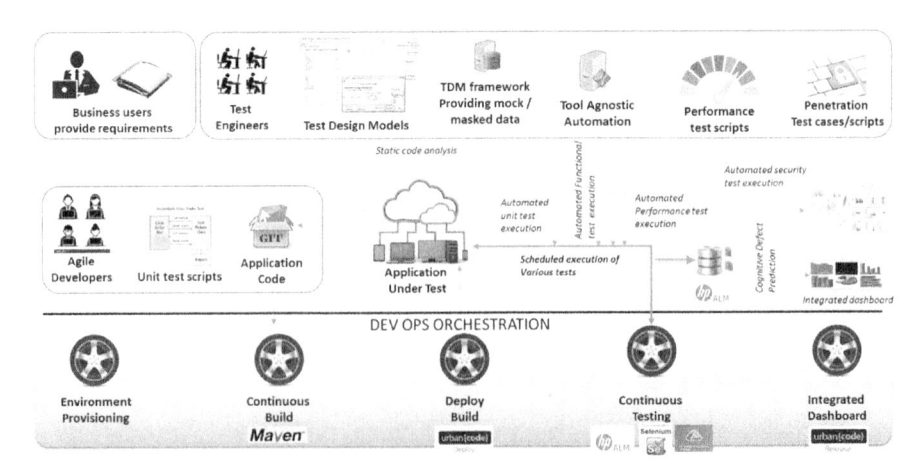

Figure 2.34: Testing Framework for Agile Projects, using DevOps Methods

117

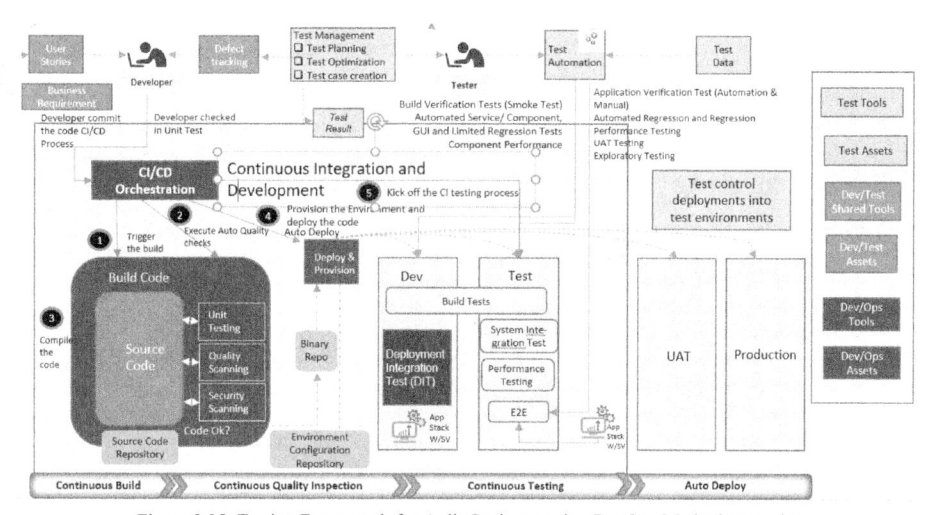

Figure 2.35: Testing Framework for Agile Projects, using DevOps Methods overview

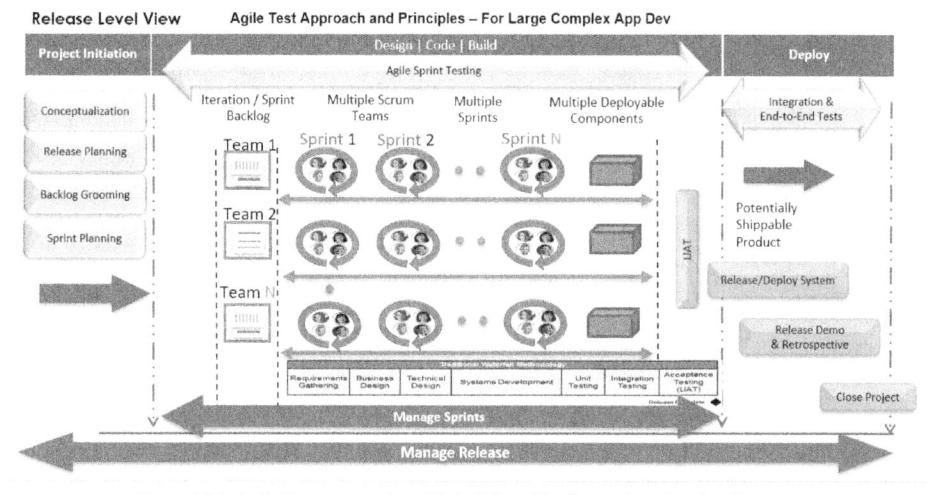

Figure 2.36: Agile Test Approach and Principles – For Large Complex App Dev

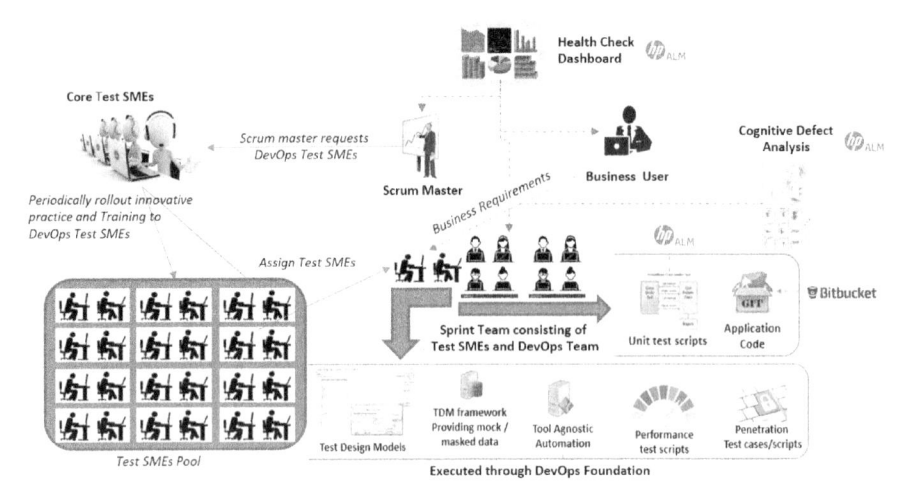

Figure 2.37: Testing Framework for Agile Projects, using DevOps Methods

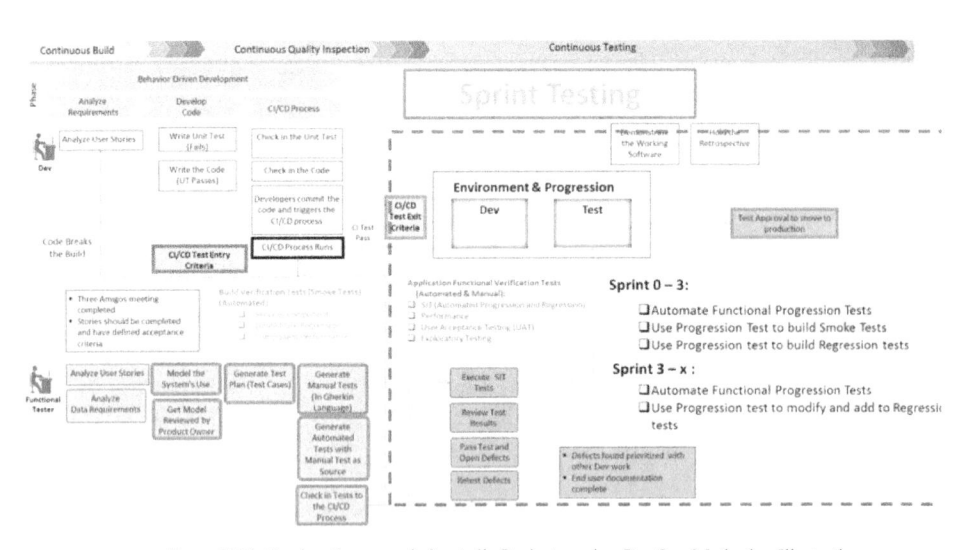

Figure 2.38: Testing Framework for Agile Projects, using DevOps Methods - Illustration

5.16. DevOps "Path to Production Model"

Illustrated view of *DevOps* tooling integration for *Path to Production* principle.

119

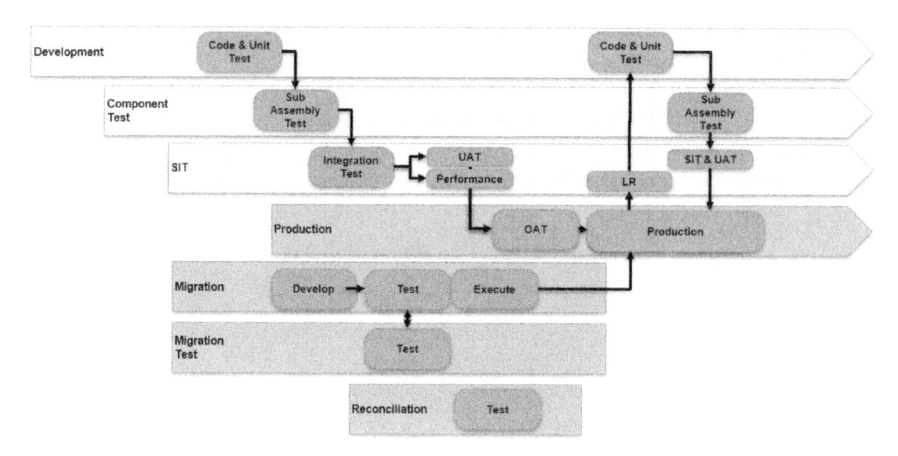

Figure 2.39: DevOps "Path to Production Model"

5.17. Process Comparisons – Traditional versus DevOps

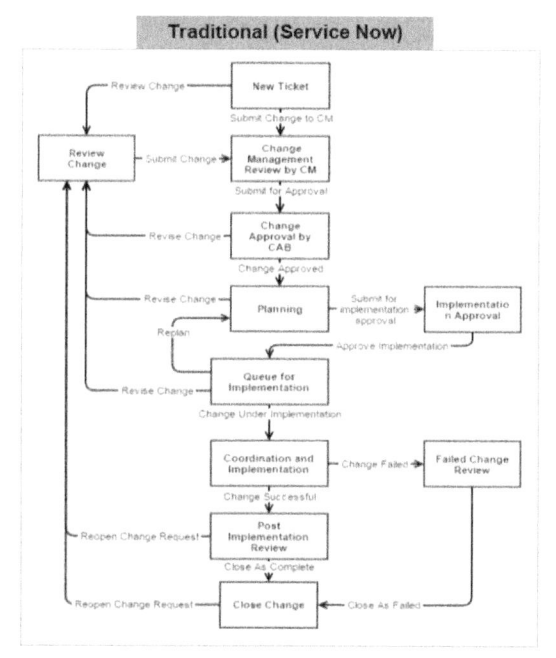

Figure 2.40: CHANGE Management: Traditional Process Overview (Standard Change)

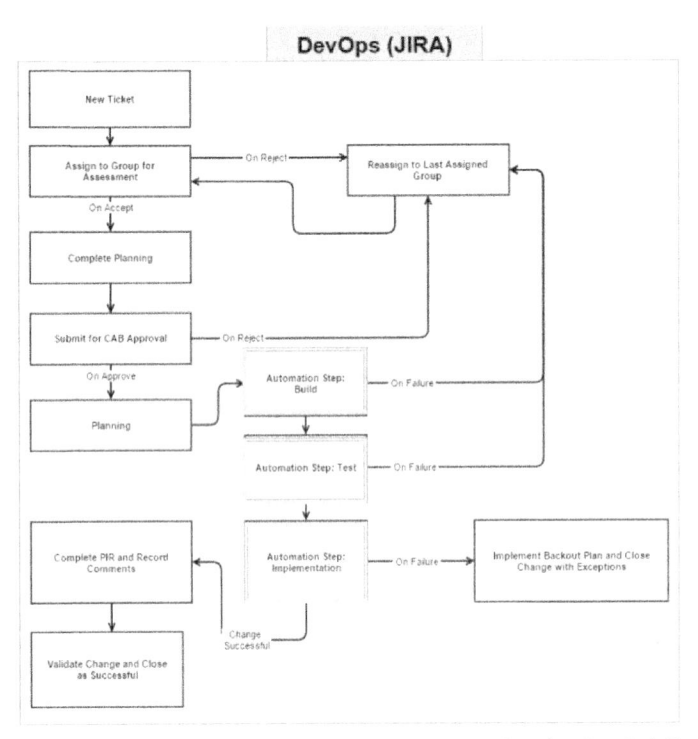

Figure 2.41: CHANGE Management: DevOps Process Overview (Standard Change)

5.18.1. Change Management Process Comparisons – Traditional versus DevOps

The following steps explain *normal* and DevOps change management process flow work:

Traditional	DevOps
When a ticket is raised, based on the matching conditions the entry criterion is verified to assign the request. By default, the request is assigned to *Change Management* group, when no conditions are matched.	When a change request is raised, based on the matching conditions, the entry criterion is verified to assign the request. When no conditions are matched, the request is assigned to *Change Management* group.
The *Change Coordinator* assesses and evaluates the request and submits the request for manager approval.	The *Release Coordination Group* assesses and evaluates the request. A plan is created to implement the request and assigned to **Change Advisory Board** (**CAB**) for approval.
The *Change Manager* performs one of the following actions on the request: • **Approve**: The request is assigned to the CAB for further assessment. • **Reject**: The request is reassigned to the change coordinator for	On approval by the CAB, the following steps are performed: • **Start Build Activity (Automated Script)**: Initiates the build script to create the software package for the release. • **Check Build Status (Automated Script)**: Verifies if the build script is

reevaluation or the request is cancelled/closed.	running successfully. If the build fails, records the build and closes the request with exceptions. • **Start Test Activity (Automated Script):** Executes the test scripts to verify if the software package works as designed. • **Check Test Execution Status (Automated Script):** Verifies if the test is successful. If the test fails, run the back out plan or update the status as test failed and close the request with exceptions. • **Start Implementation (Release Automation):** Executes the deployment script to implement the package. • **Retrieve Release Status from Release Automation:** Gathers the release information from release automation application. **Note:** If the implementation fails, run the back out plan and close the request with exceptions.
The **CAB** assesses the request with one of the following actions: • **Approve by all approvers**: The request is approved by all the CAB members. • **Approve or reject by one approver**: The request is approved by one of the CAB members. • **Urgent approve by all approvers**: The request is submitted for an urgent approval by the CAB. **Note:** The Change Manager can withdraw the request from CAB approval and can close the request during approval phase.	The request is implemented and validated for completeness. The change request is then closed by the *Release Coordination Group*.
When the **CAB** approves, the change is approved for its implementation. If not, the CAB proposes an approval with modifications to the change request.	

Traditional

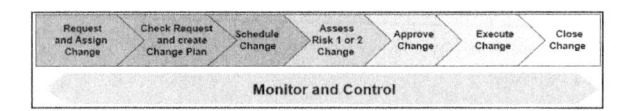

DevOps

Figure 2.42: CHANGE Management: Traditional vs DevOps Process Overview (Standard Change)

5.18.2. Quality Management Process Comparisons – Traditional vs DevOps

Quality Management: Traditional Framework

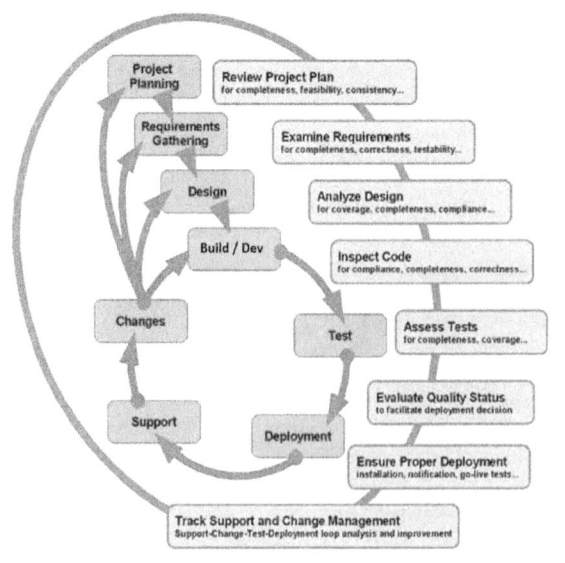

Figure 2.43: QUALITY Management: Traditional Framework Process flow

Traditional Method
- Qualitative checkpoint at every phase / level.
- Mostly manual intervention, based on baseline status.
- Automatic QA limited to *Build* and to some extent *Test* phases.

- QA through/using *Deliverables* quality approach & techniques.
- No direct integration between Development and Operations.
- Release, confirming final QA status/checkpoint (Success/Failure?).
- Sampled scenarios / projects, needing or confirming to QA status.
- QA by peer, teams, functions, clients (on their scope/phases).

Quality Management: Within DevOps Framework

Figure 2.44: QUALITY Assurance: Within / Using DevOps Framework

Within DevOps Framework

- Integral within SDLC and integrated to operations.
- Every phase confirms QA status/checkpoint (Success/Failure?).
- Automated controls for build, test and deploy lifecycles for IaaS, SaaS, PaaS.
- Automated configured QA checkpoint at every phase / level, while Deliverables QA is manually validated and certified.
- QA outcomes known, confirmed and validated between development and operations, with best automated controls.
- All scenarios and projects can easily confirm to QA status, with some exceptions of some projects on case-2-case (SaaS).
- *System QA* performed by configured automated systems and DevOps Tools, while *Manual QA* performed by teams & clients (on their scope/phases).

QUALITY Assurance: Within / Using DevOps Framework {Implementation Phase}

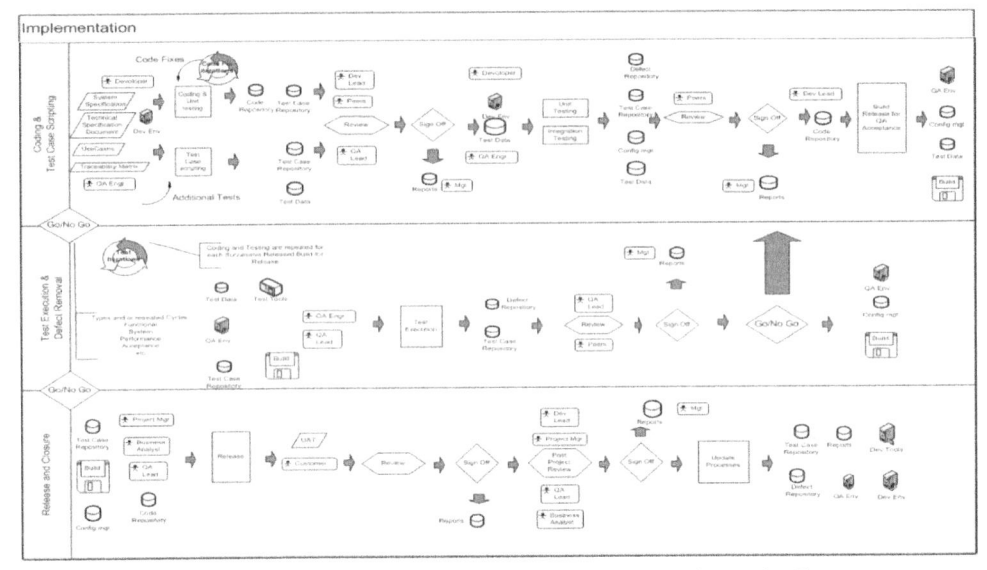

Figure 2.45: QUALITY Assurance: Using DevOps Framework - Implementation Phase

5.19. Agile vs DevOps

Agile addresses gaps in *Customer* and *Developer* communications.

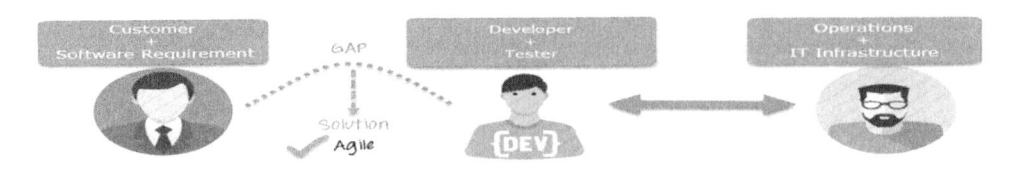

DevOps addresses gaps in Developer and IT Operations communications.

Agile	DevOps
Emphasizes breaking down barriers between developers and management / leadership.	Emphasizes breaking down barriers between software deployment teams and operation teams.
Addresses gaps between customer requirements and development teams.	Addresses gaps between development and operation teams.
Focuses more on functional and non-functional readiness.	Focuses more on operational and business readiness.
Agile development pertains mainly to the way development is thought out by the company.	Emphasizes on deploying software in the most reliable and safest ways which aren't necessarily always the fastest.
Agile development puts a huge emphasis on training all team members to have varieties of similar and equal skills. So that, when something went wrong, any team member can get assistance from any member in the absence of the team leader / SME / Architect.	DevOps, likes to divide and conquer, spreading the skill set between the development and operation teams. It also maintains consistent communication.
Agile development manages on *Sprints*. It means that the time table is much shorter (less than 30 days) and several features are to be produced and released in that period.	DevOps strives for consolidated deadlines and benchmarks with major releases, rather than smaller and more frequent ones

DevOps: Accelerating change delivery to achieve faster time to market.

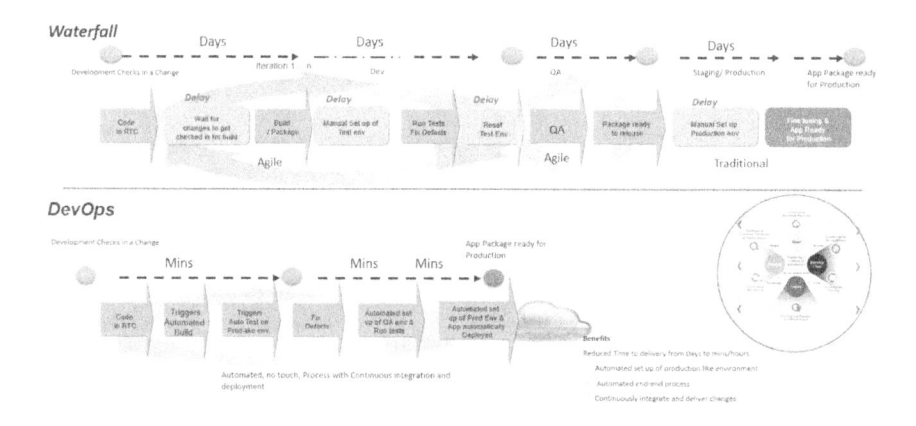

Figure 2.46: DevOps vs. Waterfall – Change Management

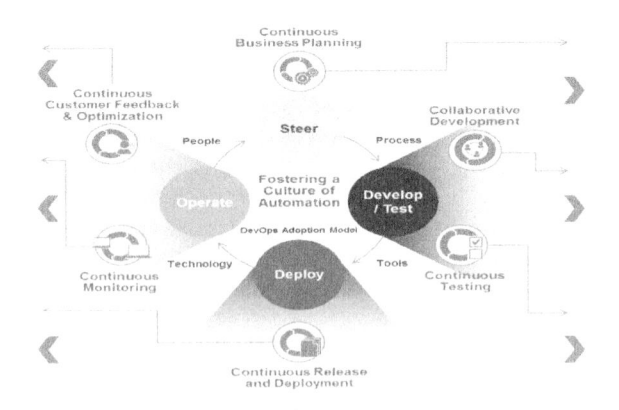

Figure 2.47: DevOps high level overview

6. DevOps Implementation – Approach and Guidelines
6.1. DevOps "Design Guiding Principles"

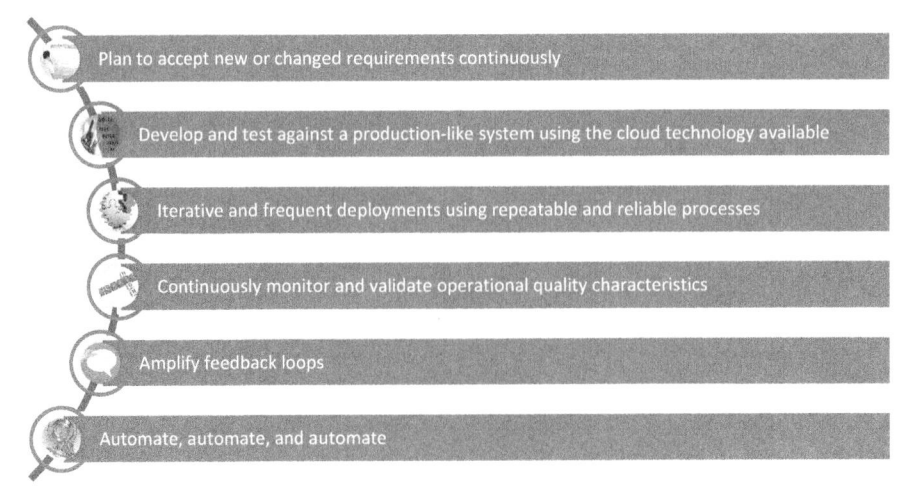

- Plan to accept new or changed requirements continuously
- Develop and test against a production-like system using the cloud technology available
- Iterative and frequent deployments using repeatable and reliable processes
- Continuously monitor and validate operational quality characteristics
- Amplify feedback loops
- Automate, automate, and automate

Figure 2.48: DevOps "Design Guiding Principles"

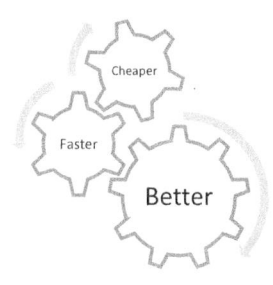

6.2. DevOps "Implementation Approach"

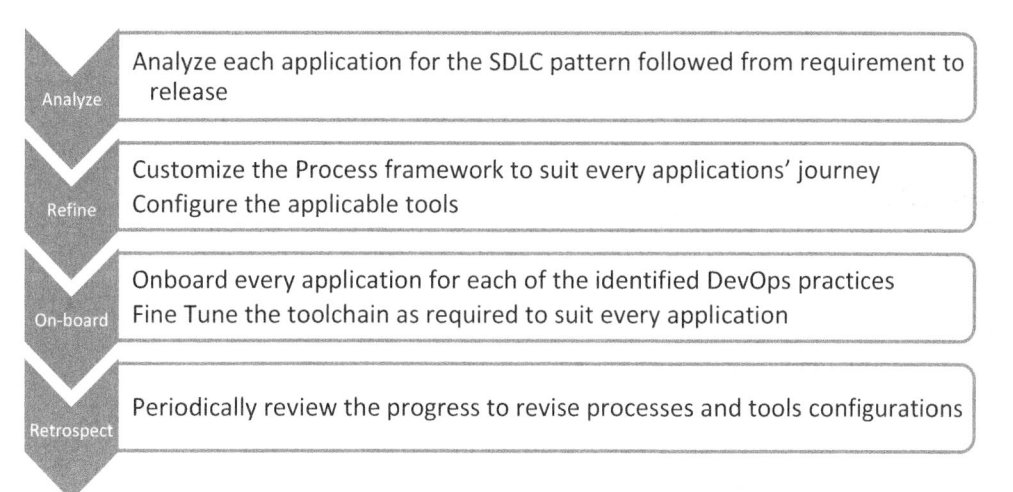

Analyze	Analyze each application for the SDLC pattern followed from requirement to release
Refine	Customize the Process framework to suit every applications' journey. Configure the applicable tools
On-board	Onboard every application for each of the identified DevOps practices. Fine Tune the toolchain as required to suit every application
Retrospect	Periodically review the progress to revise processes and tools configurations

Figure 2.49: DevOps "Implementation Approach"

6.3. DevOps "Implementation Considerations"

Content	Description
Implementation Strategy	• Once the applications are profiled for their SDLC behaviour pattern; a common set of processes, to be followed mandatorily by each of the application support team, will be defined. The tool chain may vary in future to accommodate any new application which may need a new compatible tool. • These processes will be aimed at facilitating continuous delivery objectives by adopting lean and Six Sigma principles and the necessary tools identified. Wherever required the necessary automation facilities will be availed from the vendor's cloud platform if available. • Each application has to be *on-boarded* for the continuous delivery mechanism to be followed by each and every member of the team

	ranging from the business to the IT support team which includes the vendors and the infrastructure teams as well. • The entire set of tools used in the SDLC will be supported by the PSI team for installation, configuration and day to day user support and maintenance.
Implementation Decisions & Waivers	• The following section lists the applicable implementation decisions and where agreed the waivers for existing decisions. • There are a number of solutions supplied by client vendors on either SaaS, PaaS, or IaaS model. The table in *Appendix C* lists the currently known classification of these applications. This classification may change as each of the application is studied for its detail software lifecycle. • Every application covered under the scope of the contract will be studied for deciding its lifecycle pattern and grouped together with other applications of similar nature. An entire set of processes and associated tools' usage to be followed for such applications will be documented. Such a document will form the application specific delivery from each of the system integrators. • Every business application will need to have mandatorily go through the Business planning and release management practices. • The DevOps CI, CD, and CT practices will be evaluated and implemented on a case to case basis for each of the applications. • All recommended DevOps tools are available in private environment hosted in cloud and should be used for supporting the On-premise and IaaS applications. • Any applications hosted in a SaaS environment may be expected to use the tools and processes recommended by the SaaS vendor.

6.4. DevOps Modelling "per Product Types"

Every IT System (Product/Application) project delivery goes through *Software Delivery Life Cycle* which consists of following stages:
- Business Planning
- Business & IT Requirements
- Analysis & Design
- Development
- Unit Testing
- Deployment (in various staging environments)
- Testing for functionality and NFRs
- Release Management
- Monitoring (applications and user satisfaction)

On-Premise	IaaS	PaaS	SaaS
Application	Application	Application	Application
Data	Data	Data	Data
Runtime	Runtime	Runtime	Runtime
Middleware	Middleware	Middleware	Middleware
OS	OS	OS	OS
Virtualization	Virtualization	Virtualization	Virtualization
Servers	Servers	Servers	Servers
Storage	Storage	Storage	Storage
Networking	Networking	Networking	Networking

Component can be configured within DevOps

Component managed by and within Vendor network

Figure 2.50: DevOps Modelling "per Product Types"

XaaS Type	Definition	Examples
On-Premise	*Custom Design-developed* applications using a high level language.	
IaaS	**Infrastructure-as-a-Service (IaaS)** is a form of cloud computing that provides virtualized computing resources over the Internet. It's highly standardized selective computing functionality – such as compute power, storage, archive or other basic infrastructure components.	Cisco Metapod, Microsoft Azure, **Amazon Web Services** (**AWS**).
PaaS	**Platform-as-a-Service (PaaS)** is a category of cloud computing services that provides a platform allowing *customers to develop*, *run*, *and manage applications* without the complexity of building and maintaining the infrastructure typically associated with developing and launching an *app*.	Azure, AT&T, Netsuite, Google App Engine, Force.com
SaaS	**Software-as-a-Service (SaaS)** is a software licensing and delivery model, in which software is licensed on a subscription basis and is centrally hosted. SaaS is typically accessed by users, using a thin client via a web browser.	Google Apps, Salesforce, Citrix Cisco WebEx, Office Live

6.5. DevOps "Capability Modelling per XaaS Types Components"

Table below illustrates with analysis of *DevOps Capabilities* per XaaS categories / types.
Each DevOps Capability, per XaaS type should be considered based on each component scope.

DevOps "Capabilities"	On-Premise	IaaS	PaaS	SaaS
Continuous Business Planning	Yes	Yes	Yes	Yes
Continuous Integration (CI)	Yes	Yes	Yes	No
Continuous Testing (CT)	Yes	Yes	Yes	Depends
Continuous Deployment (CD)	Yes	Yes	Yes	Depends
Continuous Environment Provisioning (CE)	Depends	Yes	Depends	Depends
Continuous Release Management (CR)	Yes	Yes	Yes	Yes
Continuous Monitoring (CM)	Yes	Yes	Yes	Yes
Continuous Optimization & User Feedback	Yes	Yes	Yes	Yes

Figure 2.51: DevOps "Capability Modelling per XaaS Types Components"

6.6. DevOps "Tools Modelling Solution"

Sr. No.	Component	Definition	Proposed Tools Suite
1	Collaborative Development	Enables team communication and integrates with DevOps tools for in context discussions.	Confluence
2	Requirements & Design	Business process reengineering	IBM Rational DOORS, IBM Blueworks Live, EA Sparx
3	Track & Plan	Work items effective tracking	HP Octane
4	Development	Enables developers to write source code usually with a developer environment.	Eclipse, Atom, Sublime Text, Swagger, etc.
5	Source Control	Source code management and versioning.	Git-Bitbucket

6	**Build**	Compile, Package, Unit-test, and preparation of software assets.	Maven
7	**Test**	Integration test, UFT, NFT, Performance test.	HP ALM, HP UFT, HP Performance Center, Blazemeter, Selenium, BrowserStack, Rapit, Cyara, CA LISA, CA TDM
8	**Continuous Integration**	A part of DevOps capability model.	Jenkins
9	**Artefact Management**	Management of the output from the build.	IBM UrbanCode Deploy
10	**Release Management**	Enables management, preparation and deployment of releases	HP Octane, IBM UrbanCode Release
11	**Deployment Orchestration**	Processes required to get the Release into Production Env.	IBM UrbanCode Deploy
12	**IT Cloud Orchestration**		IBM UrbanCode Deploy, Blue Print Designer/ Heat Engine
13	**Configuration Management**	Automatic provision of new SCM CI's (not CMDB CI's).	IBM UrbanCode Deploy, Blue Print Designer/ Heat Engine
14	**Issue Management**	Program level issues/risk management.	HP Octane ALM

6.7. DevOps Capabilities Model within "SDLC Framework"

SDLC "DevOps Framework"	DevOps "Capabilities"	Participants "To engage for Design & Implement"
Continuous Business Planning (CP)	• Capture business requirements	Business, IT managers, Vendor managers
		Business, IT managers, Vendor

	• Analyse business requirements • Prioritize business requirements • Project Planning • Measure to Project Metrics • Requirements Traceability • Dashboard portfolio measures	managers Audit, Program managers Domain Program Managers Everybody (role specific dashboards)
Collaborative Development (CD)	Release Planning Collaborative Development Configuration Management Build Management Change Management Dashboards Requirements Traceability	Business, IT managers, Vendor managers Architects, Business analysts, Developers, Test professionals Developers Developers IT managers, Vendor managers Everybody Project managers, developers, testers
Continuous Testing (CT)	Test Management and execution Test Automation Test Data Management	Program Managers, Test Managers Testers Testers, Business Analysts
Continuous Release and Deployment (CD)	Release Management Environment Management (Provisioning automation) Deployment Automation (Application, Middleware and DBs)	Domain Program Managers, Release managers Test managers, Deployment / Release managers Service & Domain Operations managers
Continuous Monitoring (CM)	Monitor Capacity and Optimize Monitor Performance and Optimize Monitor User Experience and Optimize Event and Incident Management Operational Analytics	Service & Domain Operations managers Service & Domain Operations managers Client Business managers Service & Domain Operations managers Service & Domain Operations managers

7. DevOps – Case Study 1

Facebook Dark Launching Technique

Dark launching is the process of *gradually rolling out production-ready features* to a select set of users before a full release. This allows development teams to get user *feedback early on, test bugs, and also stress test* infrastructure performance. A direct result of continuous delivery, this method of release helps in *faster, more iterative releases* that ensure that application performance does not get affected and that the release is well received by customers.

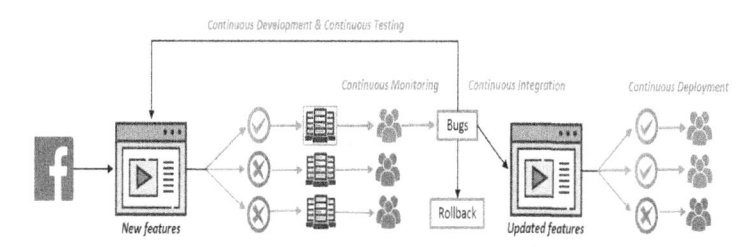

Figure 2.50: Facebook Dark Launching Technique

DEMO Application

Login use case implementation

Figure 2.51: Valid user log in

Tools and Technologies used
- Servlets/JSP using Eclipse IDE
- Tomcat as servlet container
- Git/GitHub for source code and version control repository
- Jenkins for continuous integration and delivery

- Maven for build
- Jenkins plugins
- TestNG, Selenium and Junit for unit testing
- PMD/Checkstyle for source code validation
- CatLight for monitor Jenkins job status and show notifications

Git/GitHub Repository

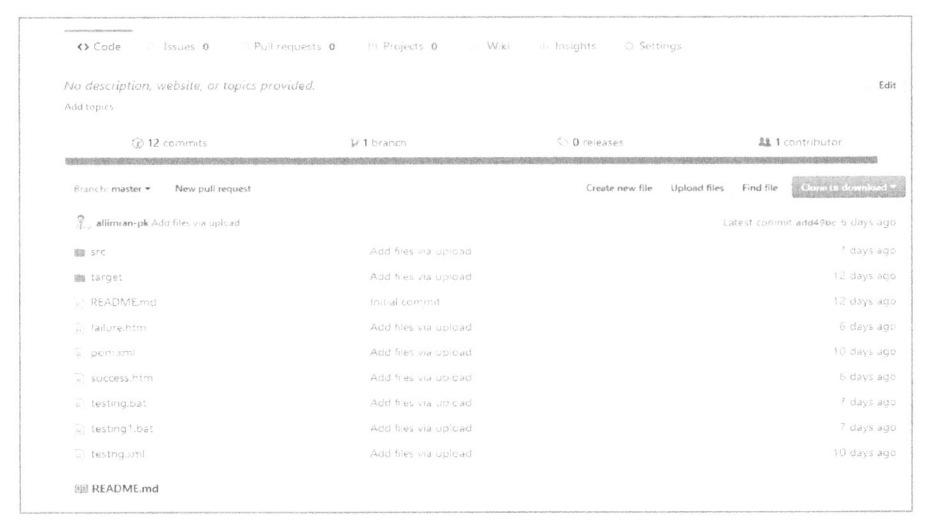

Figure 2.52: Git/GitHub Repository overview

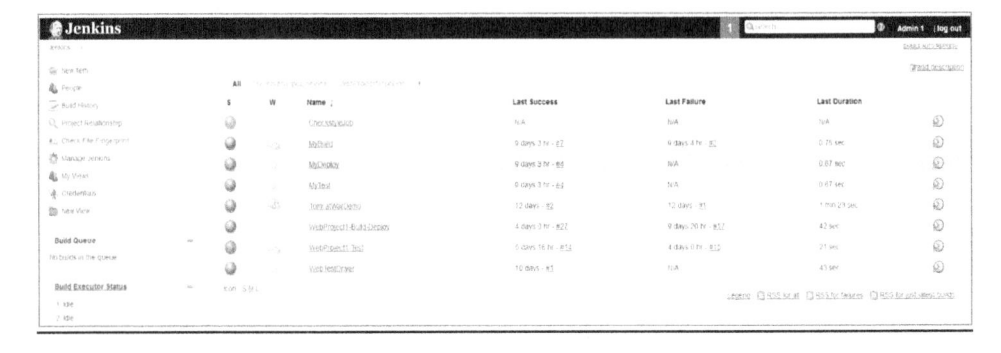

Jenkins dashboard

Figure 2.53: Jenkins dashboard overview

Delivery pipeline

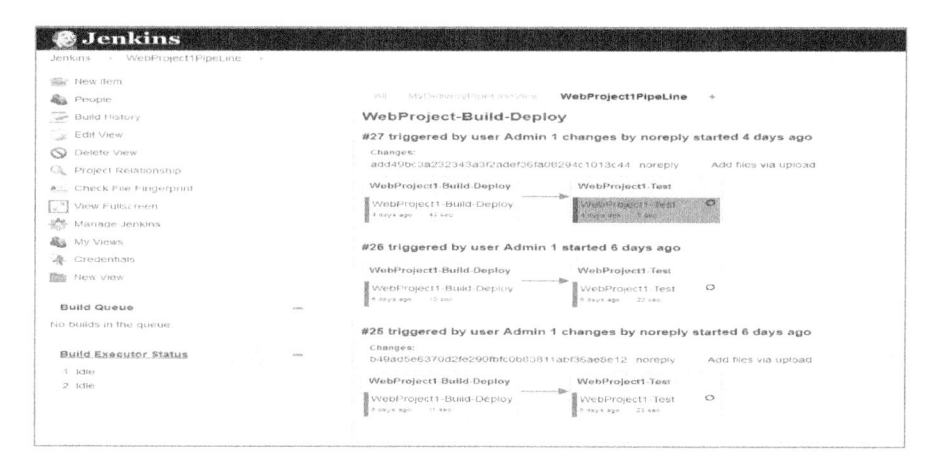

Figure 2.54: Delivery pipeline overview

Automated emails

- **Build confirmation**

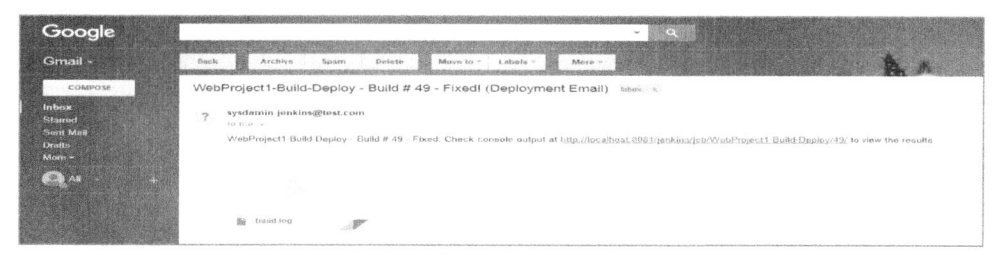

Figure 2.55: Build confirmation

- **Build failure**

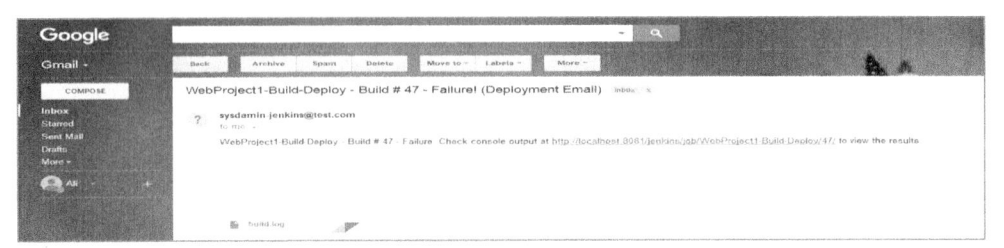

Figure 2.56: Build failure

Test execution report

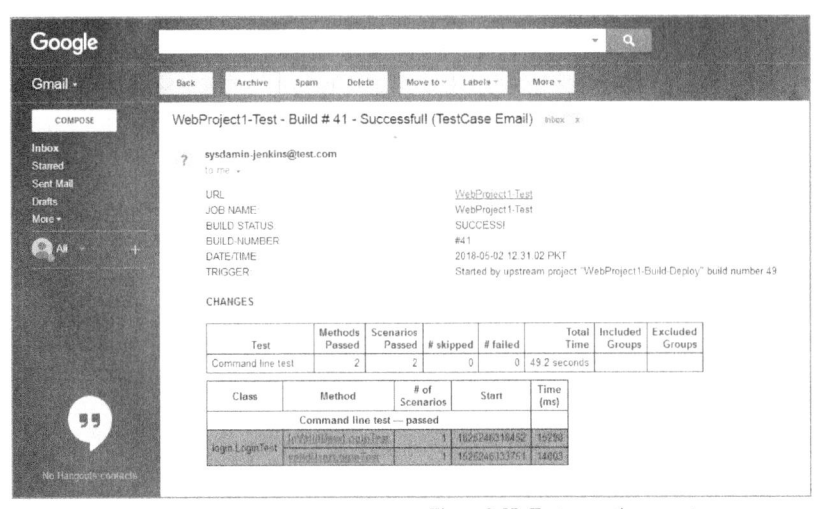

Figure 2.57: Test execution report

8. DevOps – Case Study 2

GE

The challenge

- GE Power Fleet Services development and production teams had faced an obstacle in their endeavor towards continuous improvement.

- They wanted to develop higher quality software faster, and enhance collaboration between development and production.

Requirements

- Normalize, accelerate, and automate deployments to Dev, Test, Staging, and Production environments
- Arrange, manage, and standardize release pipelines across all tools in the environment
- Build once, deploy many
- Collect release details
- Visualize the release data for stakeholders
- Build on their Continuous Integration foundation

Solution

GE Power chose the DevOps platform to automate their deployments and to compose and control their release pipelines.

Results

- Releases that took months, now take days and only 1/3 of the resources
- Higher quality software
- Removal of rework increased capacity to innovate, which improved revenue growth
- Saved 25 hours per deployment
- Critical release data helps team make quick, data-driven decisions, and measure success
- Alleviation from legacy process to release automation was accelerated

9. Appendix – Backup / References

The Leadership Suite DevOps and Business Alignment Success Guide:
https://devops.com/6-blogs-for-devops-business-alignment/

DevOps Viewpoints from Pink17:

https://devops.com/devops-viewpoints-pink17/

10 Must Read DevOps Articles to Stay in the Know:

https://www.actifio.com/company/blog/post/10-must-read-devops-articles-to-stay-in-the-know-for-2016/

5 Things DevOps is Not:

https://devops.com/what-devops-is-not/

Version Control & Code Review – SAP:

http://docs.abapgit.org/
https://github.com/larshp/abapGit

Continuous Delivery & Build – SAP:

https://medium.com/pacroy/continuous-integration-in-abap-3db48fc21028

SLACK Integration with Jenkins

https://wiki.jenkins.io/display/JENKINS/Slack+Plugin

http://www.maheshchikane.com/how-to-jenkins-build-n-deploy-slack-jenkins-integration-2/

https://stackoverflow.com/questions/30272541/jenkins-slack-integration

https://archive.sap.com/discussions/thread/3834623

https://blogs.sap.com/2015/12/13/want-to-use-bitbucket-as-your-project-repository-with-sap-web-ide/

10. Glossary

Acronym	Definition
ALM	Application Lifecycle Management
CI	Configuration Item *(related to SCM or & CMDB process)*
CI	Continuous Integration, *(a DevOps capability)*
CD	Continuous Deployment, *(a DevOps capability)*
CT	Continuous Testing, *(a DevOps capability)*
CM	Continuous Monitoring, *(a DevOps capability)*

CP	Continuous Planning, *(a DevOps capability)*
CMDB	Configuration Management Database, *(relates/refers to "Asset Management")*
CHG	Change ID, *(relates to Change management process)*
CAB	Change Advisory Board, *(relates to Change management process)*
DEV	Relates or refers to "Development"
QA	Quality Assurance
REL	Release Management Process
RFC	Request for Change
SDLC	Software Development Lifecycle
SCM	Software Configuration Management
TEST	Relates or refers to "Testing"
QC	Quality Control
QA	Quality Assurance

Figure 2.58: Terms & Acronyms

11.0. DevOps – Key Takeaways

DevOps is a cultural movement based on human and technical interactions to improve relationships and results.

DevOps is not a goal, but a never ending process of continual improvement.
--Jez Humble

What is the DevOps model?
- Integration of teams working on fixing defects and implementing change requests.

Why are we moving to DevOps model?
- Choice of prioritisation of business needs
- Increased velocity in delivering changes
- Efficiency benefits in having one team responsible for both sustain and change services
- Continuous delivery

What changes from a user perspective?
- Single queue in myIT
- Work driven by business priority (no longer SLA timelines)

- Approved change requests stay open until they are implemented
- Better transparency of where items are in the queue

What stays the same?

• DevOps requires a cultural change to improve quality and reliability.
• There are many constantly changing technical challenges facing DevOps.
• There are a number of categories of software tools, each with a number of choices.
• Cloud computing eliminates the need for expensive data centers and supporting groups.
• Information security is important to protect sensitive assets.
• Architecture is structure that defines how systems communicate and work together.
• It is important to ensure that requirements are complete and consistent.
• User acceptance test are essential to ensure that all functional requirements have been correctly implemented.

Some facts

• According to *Puppet Lab's 2015 State of DevOps Report*, "High-performing IT organizations experience 60 times fewer failures and recover from failure 168 times faster than their lower-performing peers. They also deploy 30 times more frequently with 200 times shorter lead times."

• A **Forrester report** titled *The New Software Imperative: Fast Delivery With Quality* found that *development teams that consistently deliver at the fastest cycle times enjoy the highest business satisfaction*. Importantly, teams that were able to deliver new applications the fastest were also creating the highest-quality software.

At Google:
- 15000+ engineers working on 4000+ projects
- 5500 code commits/day
- 75 million test cases are run daily
- 10 deploys per day Dev & Ops cooperation at Flickr
- Amazon deploys every 11 second on an average
- 30x more frequent deployment
- 2x the change success rate
- 12x faster Mean Time To Recover (MTTR)
- 2x more likely to exceed profitability market share & productivity goals
- 50% higher market capitalization growth over 3 years

Top predictors of IT performance

- Version control of all production artifacts
- Automated acceptance testing
- Continuous Integration & Continuous Deployment
- Peer review of production changes
- High trust culture

- Proactive monitoring of the production environment
- Win-Win relations between Dev & Ops

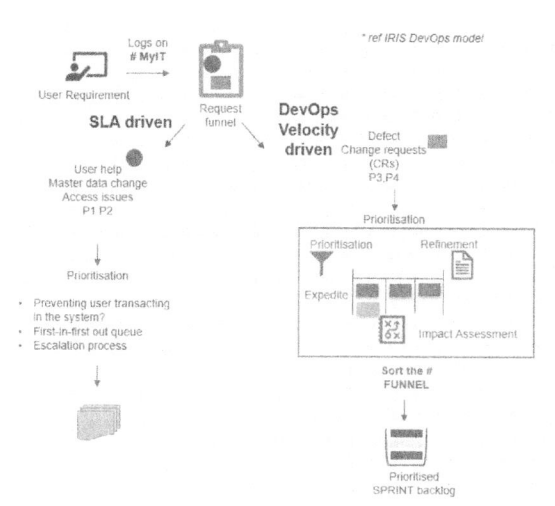

Figure 2.59: DevOps model

12.0. DevOps – Top 100 Plus DevOps Interview Questions and Answers

1. What are DevOps Goals?

- Produce smaller, more frequent software releases
- Reduce effort and risks associated with software development, transition and operation
- Improve time to market
- Better align IT responsiveness and capabilities to business needs
- Produce smaller, more frequent software releases
- Reduce effort and risks associated with software development, transition, and operation
- Improve time to market
- Improve quality of code
- Improve quality of software deployments
- Reduce cost of product iterations and delays
- Instill a culture of communication and collaboration
- Improve productivity
- Improve visibility into IT requirements and processes

2. What are important DevOps Tools used in JAVA and in SAP?

Sr. No.(s)	Phases(s)	Tool(s) JAVA	Tool(s) SAP / Cloud S/4 HANA
1	**Continuous Integration (CI)**	Jenkins	Jenkins
2	**Continuous Release and Deployment (CD)**	Jenkins	Jenkins
3	Continuous delivery and build	GIT HUB / Maven	abapGit, SCII, SLIN, ST05, SE30, ABAP Unit Code Coverage
4	Configuration management	SaltStack / Ansible, JIRA	SQA, JIRA
5	Continuous testing	HP ALM / Selenium Testing	HP ALM / Selenium Testing
6	Version control and Code review	GitLab	abapGit

3. What are 6Cs and 25 Principles of DevOps?

6Cs and 25 Principles of DevOps

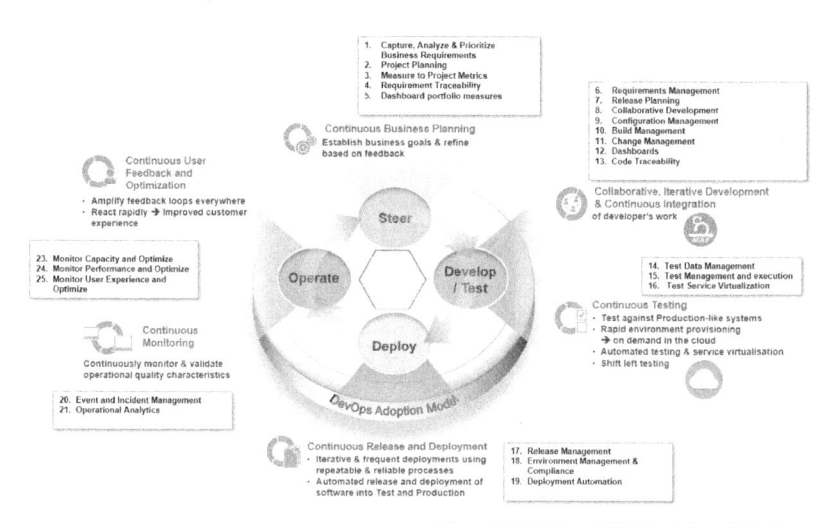

Figure 2.60: 6Cs and 25 Principles of DevOps

4. Explain one DevOps toolsets through SAP lifecycle?

DevOps toolset through lifecycle (an example – primarily SAP portfolio)

Figure 2.61: DevOps toolsets

4. Explain DevOps estimation?

DevOps estimation

Estimation Methodology

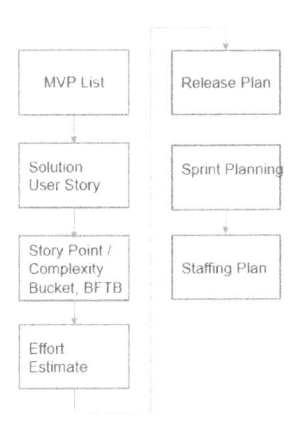

MVP List → Solution User Story → Story Point / Complexity Bucket, BFTB → Effort Estimate

Release Plan → Sprint Planning → Staffing Plan

Technical Sizing

Size	Complexity	DevOps Rating	No of Story Points
Small	Simple	1	1
Medium	Simple	2	2
Small	Intermediate	3	3
Large	Simple	4	5
Medium	Intermediate	5	8
Small	High	6	13
Large	Intermediate	7	21
Medium	High	8	34
Large	High	9	55

9 Box Estimation Model for DevOps sizing

	1	2	3
SMALL	1	2	3
	0.9	1.7	2.6
	4	5	6
Medium	5	8	13
	4.3	6.9	11.3
	7	8	9
Large	21	34	55
	18.2	29.5	47.7

Box #
Story Point
Effort (MD)

Figure 2.62: DevOps Estimation

5. Explain DevOps sample Project Plan?

30 -60 -90 Day DevOps Plan

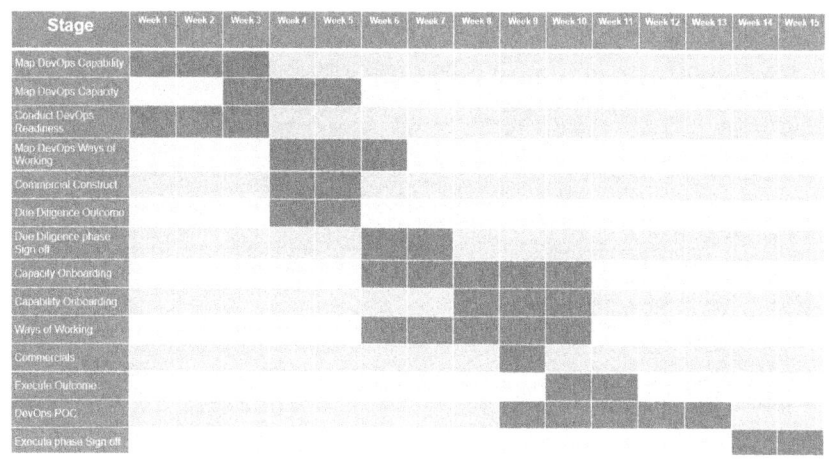

Figure 2.63: DevOps Project Plan – Example 1

6. Explain one sample DevOps meeting charter?

DevOps meeting charter

The following table presents the initial weekly schedule of DevOps activities. The Sprint duration is 2 weeks.

Activity	Participants	Time	Monday	Tuesday	Wednesday	Thursday	Friday
Triage	Virtual Team		x	x	x	x	x
Daily Stand Up	Scrum Team		x	x	x	x	x
Backlog Prioritisation	Product Owner Product Advisor Scrum Master		x				
Sprint Demo**	Scrum Teams Product Owner (Optional)				x		
Sprint Planning* & Retrospective**	Scrum Team Product Owner				x		
Change Review Board	CRB Team					x	
CRB LT Response	Leadership Team	Email					x

Figure 2.64: DevOps meeting charter – Example 1

7. Explain one sample DevOps Change review board team role and responsibilities?

Change review board Team - weekly

Change Review board	Key role
Product Owner	Agrees or assigns new business value prioritisation and approves or rejects change request
Product Advisors	Provide input to product owner regarding business value, solution context, existing user stories
	Take ownership of ticket and respond to user
Scrum Master	Provide technical inputs
SME	Consulted offline

8. Explain one sample ABAP development process?

SAP Technology stack – ABAP Development Process

Automate unit testing to verify that when code is created or changed it behaves as intended and that anything using that code will work properly as long as the unit test is passed. Tools like ABAP Unit can be used to develop and build unit tests within an SAP environment. Ideally, these tests should be executed automatically before transports are released, so the code can be verified before being moved anywhere.

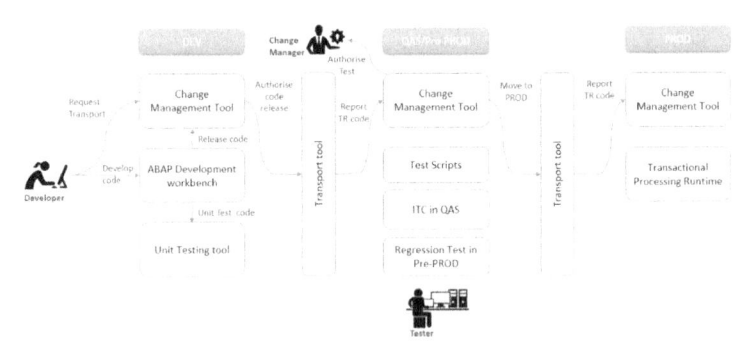

Figure 2.65: SAP development process

9. Explain DevOps Values?

DevOps is a cultural movement based on human and technical interactions to improve relationships and results.

Figure 2.66: DevOps Values - CAMS

10. Explain characteristics of DevOps Culture?

- Shared vision, goals and incentives
- Open, honest, two-way communication
- Collaboration
- Pride of workmanship
- Respect
- Trust
- Transparency
- Continuous improvement
  – Experimentation
  – Intelligent risk taking
  – Learning
  – Practicing

- Data-driven
- Safe
- Reflection
- Recognition

11. Explain automation enablers in DevOps?

- Treating infrastructure as code
- Repeatable and reliable deployment processes: CI/CD
- Development and testing performed against production-like systems
- On-demand creation of development, test, staging, and production environments
- Proactive monitoring of infrastructure components, environments, systems and services

DevOps is not just about automation but there are common enabling practices.

12. What do you mean by CI/CD in DevOps?

Continuous Integration

• Integrate the code change by each developer and run test cases

Continuous Delivery

• Taking each CI build and run it through deployment procedures on test and staging environment, so that it's ready to be deployed in production anytime.

Continuous Deployment
Continuous deployment is the next step of continuous delivery: Every change that passes the automated tests is deployed to production automatically.

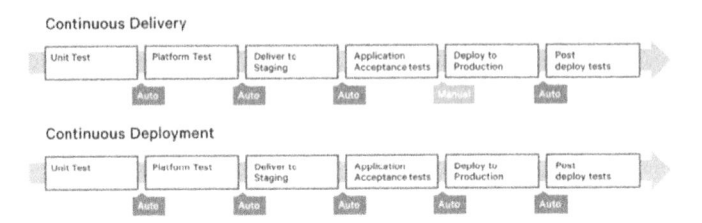

Figure 2.68: DevOps – Continuous delivery and continuous deployment

13. What you can automate in DevOps?

- Builds
- Deployments
- Tests
- Monitoring
- Self-healing
- System rollouts
- System configuration

14. What do you mean by high level DevOps Lifecycle?

•Before - pre development

Do business process reengineering to identify the functional requirements and non-functional requirements from customer perspectives.

- Security
- Backup
- Availability
- Upgradability
- Configuration management
- Monitoring
- Logging
- Metrics

- **During**
    - Communication
    - Source control
    - Automate builds
    - Automate tests
    - Automate deployments (Dev, QA, Prod)
    - System metrics

- **After - post deployment**

- Release
    - Monitor applications and systems/servers
    - Continue to run tests
    - Retrospective meetings

- Issues (yes, they do happen)
    - Post mortem

15. Can DevOps be Standalone?

No.

DevOps cannot be standalone.

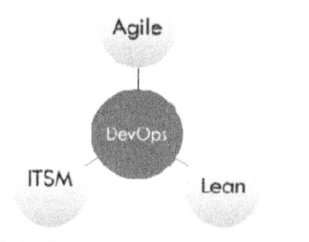

Figure 2.69: DevOps – Integration with Agile, Lean and ITSM

16. How can DevOps increase the Agility?

DevOps extends agile principles beyond the boundaries of the software to the entire delivered service.

DevOps increases agility by:

- Breaking down silos
- Improving constraints

- Taking a unified approach to systems engineering
- Applying agile principles to both Dev and Ops
- Sharing knowledge, skills, experience, and data
- Recognizing the criticality of automation
- Deploying faster with fewer errors

17. Does DevOps and Lean work together in an organization?

Yes, improving the flow of work between Dev and Ops will remove many types of waste.

18. Does DevOps and ITSM work together in an organization?

Yes, all ITSM processes will ultimately play a role in supporting DevOps by increasing flow, reducing constraints and creating business value.

Key ITSM processes that help enable DevOps include:

- Change Management
- Release and Deployment Management
- Service Asset and Configuration Management
- Knowledge Management
- Problem Management
- Incident Management
- Event Management

19. What are the desired skills in DevOps?

It may be like the following:

Desired Skills	Percentage (%)
Coding or scripting	84%
People skills – good communication and collaboration skills	60%
Business Process Reengineering skills (using Agile, Lean, ITSM)	56%
Experience with devops specific skills	19%

20. Who is DevOps Engineer?

- Currently there is no job role skill sets for a DevOps Engineer.

  These roles may be filled by:
  – Developers interested in deployment
  – System Administrators who enjoy scripting and coding

- General characteristics include someone who:
  – Can contribute / add values to business and process improvement initiatives
  – Is a good collaborator
  – Wants to be in a shared culture promoting workplace

21. Where to begin DevOps automation?

• Simplify first – don't automate bad processes
• Automate high value and repetitive tasks
• Automate error-prone work
• Automate to optimize workflow bottlenecks and communication flows
• Improve automated monitoring and notification practices, make it easy for people to do the right thing!

"Your tools alone will not make you successful."
--Patrick Debois

22. Explain precisely JIRA Software?

JIRA is a web-based open source licensed *Issue tracking system* or *Bug tracking system*. It is mainly used for agile project management. JIRA is a proprietary based tool, developed by Atlassian (www.atlassian.com). The product name 'JIRA' is shortened from the word *Gojira*, which means Godzilla in Japanese. JIRA helps us to manage the project effectively and smoothly. It is a powerful tool to track the issues, bugs, backlogs of the project. It helps the team to strive hard towards the common goal. JIRA is widely used by many organizations across the world.

Key Features of JIRA Includes:

        a. Scrum boards
        b. Project planning
        c. Project tracking
        d. Reporting
        e. Notifications

Advantages of JIRA

- Improves collaboration
- Improves tracking
- Better planning
- Increase productivity
- Improves customer satisfaction
- Flexible to use

23. Explain precisely Jenkins Software?

Jenkins is a DevOps tool for doing continuous integration and continuous delivery. For monitoring executions of repeated jobs this tool can be used. It has 100 plus plugins. Via a web interface this tool can be easily set up and can be configured. To integrate project changes more easily and access outputs for quickly identifying problems, this tool can be used.

Key Features:
• Self-contained Java-based program

- Continuous integration and continuous delivery
- Via a web interface it can be easily set up and configured
- It has more than 100 plugins
- For monitoring executions of repeated jobs this tool can be used

24. Explain precisely Docker?

An integrated technology suite enabling DevOps teams to build, ship, and run distributed applications anywhere, Docker is a tool that allows users to quickly assemble applications from components and work collaboratively. This open platform for distributed applications is appropriate for managing containers of an app as a single group and clustering an app's containers to optimize resources and provide high availability.

Key Features:

- Package dependencies with your applications in Docker containers to make them portable and predictable during development, testing, and deployment
- Works with any stack
- Isolates applications in containers to eliminate conflicts and enhance security
- Streamline DevOps collaboration to get features and fixes into production more quickly

25. Explain precisely Vagrant?

It is a DevOps Tool. To create / configure portable, lightweight, and reproducible development environments, this tool can be used. It has easy to use workflows. It focuses on automation. While setting up development environments, this tool saves DevOps teams time.

Key Features:
- No complicated setup process; on Mac OS X, Windows, or a popular distribution of Linux, just download and install it within few minutes.
- To create / configure portable, lightweight, and reproducible development environments, this tool can be used.
- While setting up development environments, this tool saves DevOps teams time.

26. Explain precisely Puppet?

It is a DevOps tool. It can be used for continuous delivery. It helps to deploy changes quickly with confidence / release better software. By decreasing cycle times, it helps to increase reliability. It helps team to become *being agile* and pays keen attention to customer needs in an automated testing environment. It ensures consistency across different boxes (like, DEV, TEST, PROD).

27. Explain precisely Chef?

It is a DevOps tool. It can be used for achieving speed, scale, and consistency by automating your infrastructure. It helps users to quickly respond to changing customer needs.

Key Features:
- Accelerate cloud adoption
- Manage data center and cloud environments
- Manage multiple cloud environments
- Maintain high availability

28. Explain precisely Ansible?

It is a DevOps tool. It can be used to speed productivity and to effectively manage complex deployments by automating the entire application lifecycle.

Key Features:

- Deploy applications
- Manage systems
- Avoid complexity
- Simple IT automation that eliminates repetitive tasks and frees teams to do more strategic work

29. Explain precisely Salt Stack?

It is a DevOps tool. It can be used for configuration management at scale. It can manage heterogeneous computing environments and can orchestrate any cloud. It can automate unique infrastructure / deployment of nearly any infrastructure and application stack used to create modern cloud, enterprise IT, and web-scale.

30. Explain precisely Visual Studio IDE?

It is a DevOps tool. It can be used for writing code accurately and efficiently while retaining the current file context in development environment for Android, iOS, web, and cloud. It can be used to refactor, identify and fix code issues. It can be used to easily zoom into details like call structure, related functions and test status. It can be used to easily develop and deploy SQL Server / Azure SQL databases with ease.

31. Explain precisely Nagios?

It is a DevOps tool. It can be used for monitoring IT infrastructure components such as applications, network infrastructure, system metrics and so on. It helps in searching log data.

32. Explain precisely RabbitMQ?

An open source multi-protocol messaging broker, RabbitMQ is a DevOps tool that supports a large number of developer platforms. RabbitMQ also runs on almost all operating systems and is easy to use.

Key Features:

• Enables software applications to connect and scale
• Gives applications a common platform for sending and reaching messages and provides a safe place for messages to sit until received
• Flexible routing, reliability, clustering, highly available queues, and more

33. Explain precisely SolarWinds Log & Event Manager?

SolarWinds offers IT management software and monitoring tools. It can be used for providing solution for security, compliance, and troubleshooting.

Key Features:

• Normalize logs to quickly identify security incidents and simplify troubleshooting
• Out-Of-The-Box rules and reports for easily meeting industry compliance requirements
• Node-based licensing
• Real-time event correlation
• Real-time remediation
• File integrity monitoring
• Licenses for 30 nodes to 2,500 nodes

34. Explain precisely Prometheus?

It is a DevOps tool. It can be used for monitoring system and time series database. Its alert system can handle notifications and silencing. It can support more than 10 languages and includes easy-to-implement custom libraries. It is popular with teams using Grafana.

35. Explain precisely Ganglia?

Ganglia provides DevOps teams with cluster and grid monitoring capabilities. This scalable tool is designed for high-performance computing systems like clusters and grids. Ganglia makes use of XML, XDR, and RRD tools.

Key Features:

• Scalable distributed monitoring system based on a hierarchical design targeted at federations of clusters
• Achieves low per-node overheads for high concurrency
• Can scale to handle clusters with 2,000 nodes

36. Explain precisely Splunk?

It is a DevOps tool. It can be used for delivering operational intelligence to teams. It can help companies to gain more security and productivity in competitive market.

It helps in delivering a central, unified view of IT services. It helps in next-generation monitoring and analytics solution. It can adapt thresholds dynamically, can highlight discrepancies and can detect areas of impact.

37. Explain precisely Sumo Logic?

Sumo Logic helps leading companies analyze and make sense of log data. DevOps teams choose Sumo Logic because it combines security analytics with integrated threat intelligence for advanced security analytics with deep insights for modern applications.

Key Features:

- Build, run, and secure AWS, Azure, or Hybrid applications
- Cloud-native, machine data analytics service for log management and time series metrics
- One platform for real-time continuous intelligence
- Remove friction from your application lifecycle

38. Explain precisely Log Stash?

It is a DevOps tool. It can be used for server side of data processing and it can dynamically transform & prepare data no matter its format or complexity. It can collect, parse, and transform logs. Here, pipelines are multipurpose and may be sophisticated to give you full visibility when monitoring deployments or even an active Logstash node.

39. Explain precisely Loggly?

It is a DevOps tool. It can be used to simplify cloud log management and for quick & efficient resolution of operational issues. It can be used to enhance customer delight by delivering good quality code of deliverables. It may use open protocols rather than proprietary agents to send logs. It can provide effective solutions helping businesses access, manage and analyze log data across the entire application stack on AWS.

40. Explain precisely Paper trail?

It is a DevOps tool. It can be used for instant log visibility and to realize value from logs you already collect. It can be used to tail & search using a browser, command-line, or API. It can be used to aggregate (all app logs, logfiles, and syslog in one place). It can also be used to react and analyze (get instant alerts, detect trends, and archive forever).

41. Explain precisely Apache ActiveMQ?

It is a DevOps tool. It can be used for high-performance clustering, client-server, peer-based communication. It is fast, and fully supports JMS 1.1 and J2EE 1.4. It can support several cross language clients and protocols.
It can be easily embedded into Spring applications. It can be configured using Spring's XML configuration mechanism. It supports advanced features like message groups, virtual destinations, wildcards, and composite destinations.

42. Explain precisely Squid?

As a cache proxy for the web, Squid is a DevOps tool which optimizes web delivery and supports HTTP, HTTPS, FPT, and more. By reducing bandwidth and improving response times via caching and reusing frequently-requested web pages, Squid also operates as a server accelerator.

Key Features:

- Extensive access controls
- Runs on most available operating systems including Windows
- Licensed under the GNU GPL
- Improves performance by optimizing data flow between client & server
- Caches frequently-used content to save bandwidth

43. Explain precisely MCollective @Puppetize?

It is a DevOps tool, it is useful while teams are working with large number of servers or working with parallel job execution systems or involved in building orchestration in server. It can use a rich data source, can perform real time discovery across the network.

44. Explain precisely CF Engine?

CF Engine helps us to do configuration management. This tool is very much helpful to automate large scale complex infrastructure. It is written in C. It is an open source configuration solution.
A DevOps tool for IT automation at web scale, CF Engine is ideal for configuration management and helps teams automate large-scale, complex, and mission-critical infrastructure. With CF Engine, you can ensure compliance even while securely making consistent global changes. It is scalable.

45. Explain precisely Gradle?

Delivering adaptable, fast automation for teams using DevOps, it accelerates productivity of developer. It helps DevOps team to deliver faster, better, cheaper Software deliverables. Developer can code in any languages here, like, Python, C++, JAVA. It has rich API and many plugins.

Key Features:

- It accelerates productivity of developer.
- It helps DevOps team to deliver faster, better, cheaper Software deliverables.
- It has rich API and many plugins.
- Developer can code in any languages here, like Python, C++, JAVA.

46. Explain precisely Jfrog Artifactory?

JFrog is enterprise-ready repository manager. It is language independent as well as technology independent.

It can be integrated with all major DevOps and CI/CD tools. It can be used for end to end tracking of artifacts from development till production.

Key Features:

• Enterprise-ready repository manager
• It can be integrated with all major DevOps and CI/CD tools. It can be used for end to end tracking of artifacts from development till production

47. Explain precisely Pros and Cons of Puppet?

Pros:

• Well-established support community through Puppet Labs
• It has the most mature interface and runs on nearly every OS
• Simple installation and initial setup
• Most complete Web UI in this space
• Strong reporting capabilities

Cons:

• For more advanced tasks, you will need to use the CLI, which is Ruby-based (meaning you'll have to understand Ruby).
• Support for pure-Ruby versions (rather than those using Puppet's customized DSL) is being scaled back.
• Because of the DSL and a design that does not focus on simplicity, the Puppet code base can grow large, unwieldy, and hard to pick up for new people in your organization at higher scale.
• Model-driven approach means less control compared to code-driven approaches.

48. Explain precisely Pros and Cons of Chef?

Pros:

• Rich collection of modules and configuration recipes.
• Code-driven approach gives you more control and flexibility over your configurations.
• Being centered around Git gives it strong version control capabilities.
• *Knife* tool (which uses SSH for deploying agents from workstation) eases installation burdens.

Cons:

• Learning curve is steep if you're not already familiar with Ruby and procedural coding.
• It's not a simple tool, which can lead to large code bases and complicated environments.
• It doesn't support push functionality.

49. Explain DevOps Best Practices – Tools perspective?

•Automated testing
•Integrated Configuration Management
•Integrated Change Management
•Continuous Integration

•Continuous Deployment
•Application Monitoring
•Automated Dashboards

50. Explain DevOps Best Practices – high level?

• Break Silos in IT
• Adjust performance reviews
• Create real-time visibility
• Use software automation wherever you can
• Choose tools that are compatible with each other
• Start with pilot projects
• Continuously deploy applications
• Create a service environment within the company
• Understand the collaboration and shared tools strategy for the Dev, QA, and infrastructure automation teams
• Use tools to capture any request
• Use agile kanban project management for automation and devops requests that can be dealt with in the tooling
• Use tools to log metrics on both manual and automated processes
• Implement test automation and test data provisioning tools
• Perform acceptance test for each deployment tooling
• Ensure continuous feedback between the teams to spot gaps, issues, and inefficiencies
• Build the right culture and keep the momentum going: Once you start your DevOps process, continue to improve and refine it
• Focus on culture not the tools
• Conduct version control and automation
• Create tight feedback loops
• Participate in DevOps Community
• Redefine your skill sets: The most salient skills their respondents say they look for in hiring for their DevOps teams are coding and scripting (84%), people skills (60%), process re-engineering skills (56%) and then experience with specific tools (19%).

51. Explain DevOps in a Nutshell?

For most enterprises, increasing the speed of deployment is a key goal of their DevOps initiatives. In order to achieve that goal, they often deploy technology that promises to speed development and they frequently implement Agile development techniques, such as test-driven development, continuous integration, pair programming, and Scrum methodologies. Experts say it's important for organizations to remember that the techniques and the technology aren't the goal in themselves; instead, they are a means for accomplishing goals like faster deployment, improved code quality and, ultimately, better support for the business.

52. Explain DevOps flow in a Nutshell?

• Create issue in Jira
• Commit changes to Bitbucket
• Code is pushed to Gerrit

- Code review done
- Gerrit pushes to Bitbucket
- Jenkins checks out, compile, package, run unit test
- Jenkins create docker image and deploys container to QA server
- Jenkins pushes image to registry
- Jenkins pushes artifacts to artifactory

53. Explain critical success factors of DevOps?

- Management commitment to culture change
- Creation of a collaborative, learning culture
- Common values and vocabulary
- Systems engineering that spans Dev and Ops
- Meaningful metrics
- A balance between automation and human interaction
- Application of agile and lean methods
- Open and frequent communication

54. What is Virtualization? Explain its benefits.

Virtualization
Software is used to mask the physical implementation of an environment (servers, networks, data sources, and so on.) to optimize the use of resources.

Benefits
- Enables more efficient use of physical resources
- More flexibility of deciding when and how to deploy
- Can help provide higher resiliency and scalability
- Enables advanced DevOps practices such as automation, rollbacks, reduced MTTR, and so on

55. What are Virtualization types?

- Hardware (Server) Virtualization
- Storage Virtualization
- Data Virtualization
- Service Virtualization
- Network Virtualization
- Desktop & User Virtualization
- Application Virtualization.

56. What is Tivoli Service Automation Manager?

It enables users to request, deploy, monitor, and manage cloud computing services with traceable processes.

57. What is SoftLayer Portal?

Ability to order and interact with products and services, manage, and maintain SoftLayer account.

https://www.youtube.com/watch?v=gscUrEL3IT8&list=PL6j6__J0kCu_yfau-LShdnZCOhFYh-RZa

58. What is Technical debt? Why it is important?

Technical debt is the cost of not making improvements to your environment which, over time, results in:

• Learn principles for attaining continuous operations capabilities
• Understand the shared duties between development and operations
• Improve team awareness and proactive involvement in monitoring the codebase, test suite, application, infrastructure, and so on.
• Discover helpful resources to continue learning more about operations for infrastructures implementing DevOps continuous operations, and continuous delivery applications.

59. Explain types of Operational Technical Debt?

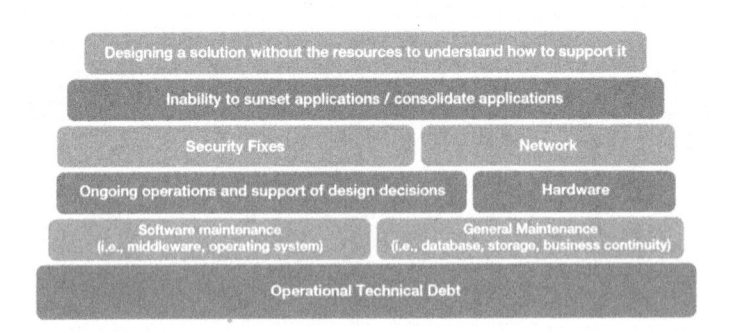

Figure 2.70: Operational Technical Debt Types

60. What is Gold Plating?

Gold Plating is working on a task beyond the point where the extra effort is worth any value it adds.

61. What is the cultural challenge for DevOps?

People need to work together across traditional role boundaries. Developers need to work with operations and testing teams.

62. At which phase would container management tools be required?

Containers are created in the packaging phase.

63. What is Infrastructure as a Service (IaaS)?

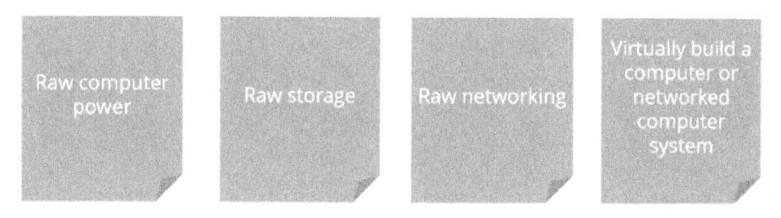

Figure 2.71: IaaS Overview

Payment is for resources provisioned:
- When you use a component, no one else can use it
- Fair to pay for components requested even if unused
- Main difference is that virtual components are easy to return to the Cloud vendor
    - Short term *rental* can be very economic
    - Easy to reconfigure to smaller or larger computers

64. What is Platform as a Service (PaaS)?

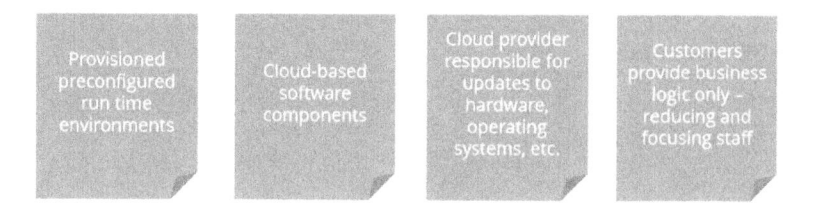

Figure 2.72: PaaS Overview

Payment is for resources used.

65. What is Software as a Service (SaaS)?

Figure 2.73: SaaS Overview

- Pay for actual usage
  - Message sent/received
  - Storage of information
  - Other factors

66. What is an example of IaaS?

IaaS provides raw computing, storage, and networking.

67. What is segregation of duty?

Require several entities to complete a sensitive operation.

68. What are the differences between Architecture versus design?

Architecture	Design
Strategic design	Tactical design
Global –"how"	Local –"what"
Programming paradigms, architectural patterns	Algorithms, design patterns, programming idioms
Non-functional requirements	Functional requirements
Represented in UML as component, deployment, and package diagrams	Represented in UML as class, object, and behaviour diagrams which appear in detailed functional design documents

69. What do you mean by Client Server Architecture?

Client server architecture utilizes a thick client communicating with data storage.

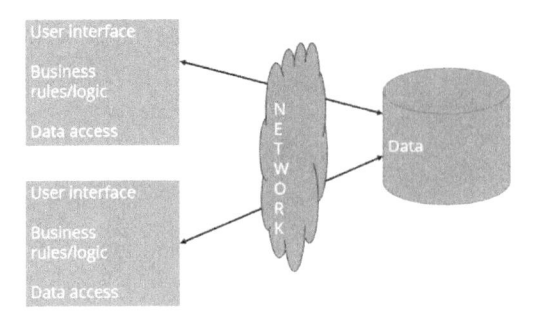

Figure 2.74: Client Server architecture overview

70. What are the advantages of Client Server Architecture?

Advantages

- Separation of user interface presentation and business logic processing from the centralized data layer
- Reusability of server components
- Ease of managing security of centrally located data
- Optimize infrastructure usage
- Scalable

71. What are the disadvantages of Client Server Architecture?

Disadvantages

- Lack of infrastructure for dealing with requirements changes
- Security
- Server availability and reliability as it is a single point of failure
- Testability and scalability
- Presentation and business logic in same place.

72. What are the advantages of Service Oriented Architecture?

Advantages

- Loose coupling
- Interoperability—business services across platforms
- Location transparency
- Reuse of IT Services—can expose legacy applications
- Development cost reductions
- Speed to market
- Better business and IT integration.

73. What are the disadvantages of Service Oriented Architecture?

Disadvantages

- Costly to migrate
- Need good control system
- Requires complex service auditing and monitoring
- Additional development and design.

74. What do you mean by 4+1 Architecture View Model?

The 4+1 architecture view model describes the architecture in terms of four different views:

- Logical view is end user functionality
- Development view is software management
- Process view is system processes and communication
- Physical view or deployment view is software topology on hardware
- The resulting scenarios or use cases form the +1 view.

75. Define Architecture?

Architecture is infrastructure which interconnects system components. It is often realized as messaging system and associated systems.

76. What are the features of effective user stories?

• Agile development often specify requirements in terms of user stories
• Effective user stories need to be testable

• Features of effective user stories are as follows:

- It needs to describe an action which has value to a specific user
- It needs to target a specific user or role
- It needs to have clearly stated acceptance criteria which can easily be tested
- It needs to be small enough to implement in a few days
- It needs to be short and precise

77. Give examples of Technical Debt user stories?

As an application owner, *I want to* upgrade the DB2 version of my application so that I have the most current product capabilities and avoid outages and performance degradation that there are known fixes or improvements for.

As an application owner, I need an archival process for data over 1 year old so that I can reduce the size of my database by xx%, which will save "x" dollars per month and improve transaction performance by xx%.

As an application owner, I want to apply the "xxx" security patch to my infrastructure so that IBM is not in the news as being hacked and there is not a negative impact on the stock price.

As a support team member for a Domain, I need a consolidated view of log information in the form of a portal so that we improve problem resolution time by xx%.

78. Define Mean Time To Recover (MTTR)?

The ability to execute successful end-to end business transactions.
After problem identification, how long does it take to:

- Find the root cause
- Recreate the issue in development
- Design / Code and Test Solution
- Deploy fixed component or feature back into Production.

79. Explain Functional Test Types?

Business goals fulfillment is the main purpose of functional test cases.

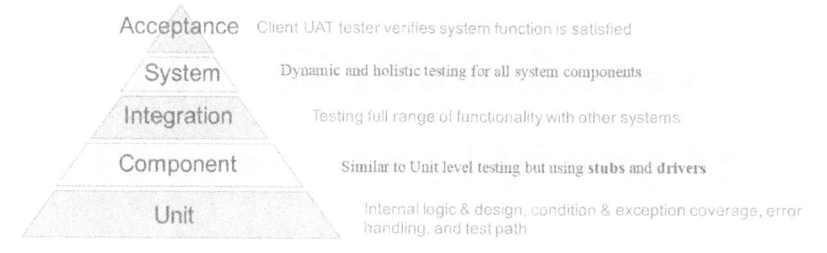

- **Acceptance**: Client UAT tester verifies system function is satisfied
- **System**: Dynamic and holistic testing for all system components
- **Integration**: Testing full range of functionality with other systems
- **Component**: Similar to Unit level testing but using **stubs** and **drivers**
- **Unit**: Internal logic & design, condition & exception coverage, error handling, and test path

Figure 2.75: Functional test types

80. Explain Non-Functional Test Types?

Performance, resource utilization, usability, compatibility etc. fulfillment is the main purpose of Non--functional test cases.

Non-Functional Tests

- Performance
- Usability
- Compatibility
- Security
- Compliance
- Resiliency

Figure 2.76: Non Functional test types

81. Explain Software Testing Principles?

1. Testing shows presence of defects
2. Exhaustive testing is impossible
3. Early testing
4. Defect clustering
5. Pesticide Paradox

6. Testing is context dependent
7. Absence--of--errors fallacy.

82. Explain DevOps Testing Pillars?

DevOps Testing

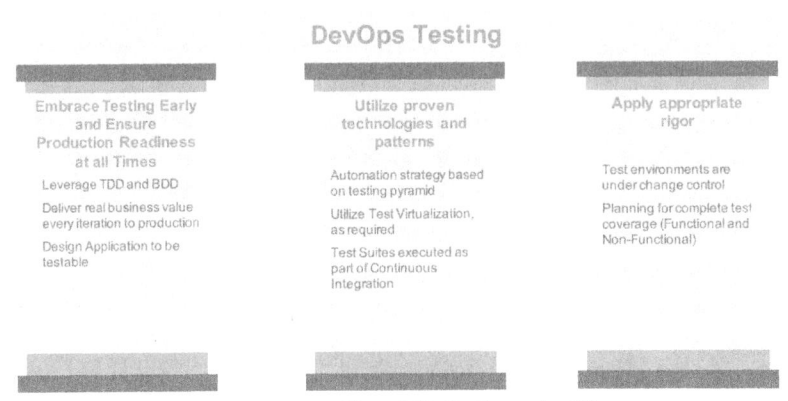

Embrace Testing Early and Ensure Production Readiness at all Times
- Leverage TDD and BDD
- Deliver real business value every iteration to production
- Design Application to be testable

Utilize proven technologies and patterns
- Automation strategy based on testing pyramid
- Utilize Test Virtualization, as required
- Test Suites executed as part of Continuous Integration

Apply appropriate rigor
- Test environments are under change control
- Planning for complete test coverage (Functional and Non-Functional)

Figure 2.77: DevOps testing Pillars

83. Explain test coverage?

It is a measure of how much of executable code was tested.

84. Explain Myths of Test Coverage?

Myth: Test coverage = Quality Target
Reality: Test coverage helps find untested code

Myth: A test suite that passes without any failures is indicative of high quality code **Reality:** Cannot guarantee that all of the code is tested by test suite

Myth: A good measure for test suite quality is code coverage achieved by tests **Reality:** Even with 100% code coverage and all tests passing, there can be undiscovered bug

85. Explain Black Box Testing?

Testing method where the internal structure / design is NOT known to the tester.

86. Explain White Box Testing?

Testing method where the internal structure / design is known to the tester.

87. What are the differences between Black Box Testing and White Box Testing?

Black Box Testing	White Box Testing
Applicable to higher levels of testing (e.g., acceptance, integration & system).	Applicable to lower levels of testing (e.g., mainly unit, component, some integration & system).
Programming knowledge not Required.	Programming knowledge required.
User stories / specifications used as basis for test cases .	Detail design / code used as basis for test cases (inputs, outputs).
• All-pairs Testing • Orthogonal Array /Combinatorial Testing	• Branch (Decision) • Path • Full Regression • Statement

88. How do we know when to start testing?

Test begins when the project begins. For example: TDD, BDD

89. How do we know when to stop testing?

- Don't stop testing --Assess production readiness for iteration
- Risk assessment for any deviations from plan/standard process
- Thoroughness measures – code/risk coverage
- Cost & iteration boundary
- Reached an explicit level of testing

90. Define Modular Testing Framework?

- Independent scripts aligned to module structure of application being tested
- Modules used hierarchically to build larger test cases

91. Explain advantages of Modular Testing Framework?

- Quick startup
- Enables changes at lowest levels as not to impact other test cases

92. Explain disadvantages of Modular Testing Framework?

Data is embedded in the test script, maintenance is difficult.

93. Define Data Driven Testing Framework?

- Test input and expected results are stored in a separate file usually in tabular format
- A single script can execute with multiple sets of data
- Driver script navigates through program, reads data input and logs test status

94. Explain advantages of Data Driven Testing Framework?

Reduces the number of test scripts required (over Modular).

95. Explain disadvantages of Data Driven Testing Framework?

Tight coupling between scripts and data may exist.

96. Define Keyword Driven Testing Framework?

- Utilizes data tables and self-explanatory keywords that describe actions
- Test data stored separately just like the Keywords/Actions (Directives)
- Keyword Driven Testing separates test creation process into two distinct stages:
    1. Design & development stage
    2. Execution stage

97. Explain advantages of Keyword Driven Testing Framework?

Both data and keywords can be reused across scripts providing flexibility.

98. Explain disadvantages of keyword driven Testing Framework?

Increased flexibility can drive complexity.

99. Define Hybrid Testing Framework?

- Combination of modular, data driven and keyword driven frameworks.
- Data driven scripts can access information provided by keyword driven approach

100. Explain advantages of Hybrid Testing Framework?

Incorporates all testing framework approaches.

101. Explain disadvantages of Hybrid Testing Framework?

Most complex approach

102. Explain Penetration (PEN) Test?

Uses ethical hacking techniques to penetrate an application for the purpose of finding security vulnerabilities that a malicious hacker could potentially exploit.

103. Explain test automation myths?

Myth: Every manual test can/should be automated.

Reality: Consider cost savings and make tradeoff.

Myth: Test automation is just a matter of purchasing the *right* tool.
Reality: Rare that an off the shelf tool will meet all requirements.

Myth: Test automation always leads to cost savings.
Reality: Time to train test teams, documenting test cases, learning test tools are sometimes not considered.

NOTES

NOTES

13.0. DevOps all-Inclusive Self-Assessment Checklist featuring more than 100 new and updated real-time business case-based questions

A) Introduction

DevOps - Stage	DevOps - Framework	DevOps - Capabilities
Steer	Continuous Business Planning	- Capture, Analyse & Prioritize Business Requirements - Project Planning - Measure to Project Metrics - Traceability - Dashboard portfolio measures
Develop	Collaborative Development	- Release Planning - Collaborative Development - Configuration Management - Build Management (Requires Integration with Build automation) - Change Management - Dashboards - Traceability
Test	Continuous Testing	- Test Management and execution - Test Automation - Test Data Management
Release & Deploy	Continuous Release and Deployment	- Release Management - Environment Management (provisioning automation) - Deployment Automation (Application, Middleware and Databases)
Operate	- Continuous Monitoring - Continuous Feedback and Optimization	- Monitor Capacity and Optimize - Monitor Performance and Optimize - Monitor User Experience and Optimize

		• Event and Incident Management • Operational Analytics

B) **Current Tools**

SDLC Stage	Tool being used	Tool capabilities being used	Integrated with ?	Client Mandated ?	Where is the Tool Hosted? (Client/ Organization/ Local)	Reference
Project planning/ Requirements						
Develop						
Test						
Deploy & Release						
Monitor						
User Feedback & Optimize						

C) **Continuous business planning**

Question	DevOps Capability	DevOps Score Guideline	Score	Actual score	Actual Finding	Does it business critical?	DevOps Recommendation
How are the requirements captured ?	-Capture, analyse, prioritize business requirements	-Requirements are integrated with other DevOps attributes e.g. continuous testing, continuous monitoring. -Requirements are in tools and cross-linked with other deliverables e.g. FS, TS, PDD. -Requirements are in tools like Remedy, Service Now,	4 3 2				

		requirements stored in Solman as a stand-alone document. -Word/Excel documents and communication is through mail only	1				
Have the Requirements been collected using Design thinking principles ?	Capture, analyse, prioritize business requirements	All or most of design thinking principles are used like • Silent brainstorming • Affinity mapping • Five Whys root cause analysis • So what? impact analysis • Value stream mapping • Personas • Empathy mapping • Scenario mapping • Assumption mapping • Sharing of design research data within the team.	4				
			3				
		-Most of the	2				

		design thinking principles are followed.					
		-A few Design thinking principles e.g. scenario mapping, empathy mapping are used.	0				
		-No Design thinking principle used					
How are the requirements prioritized ?	Capture, analyse, prioritize business requirements	-Prioritization is done using requirements management tools like SNOW, SolMan, JIRA and integrated with other ALM tools.	4				
		-Prioritization is done using requirements management tools like SNOW, SolMan, JIRA without any integration to other ALM tools.	3				
		-Prioritization is done using excel sheets/ MS project and conducting stakeholder meetings.	1				
		-No	0				

		prioritization.					
How are the project activities planned ?	Project planning	-Project planning is done in Agile way using tools like SolMan 7.2 with focussed build.	4				
		-Project planning is done in Agile way using tools like MS project.	3				
		-Project planning is done in waterfall way using SolMan.	2				
		-Project planning is done in waterfall way using MS project.	1				
		-Adhoc project plans with high level delivery dates only.	0				
Are any metrics defined ?	Measure to project metrics	-Metrics are well defined and data collected and analysed using tools like Solution Manager.	4				
		-Partial metrics data collection for test and defect management, productivity etc. using tools	3				

		like Solution Manager, HP-ALM, "Clear Quest".	2				
		-Metrics collected and analysed using manual methods in excel sheets and automated reports generated through automation in excel sheet.	1				
		-Metrics are defined and collected on adhoc basis and need basis for management reports.	0				
		-No metrics					
Do you have end-to-end Requirements Traceability?	Traceability	-Automated Traceability using integrated SolMan 7.2 with other tools.	4				
		-Traceability using SolMan, release are very well planned and tracked but manual updates.	3				
		-Traceability using excel sheet or home grown tools, release are very well	2				

		planned and tracked but manual updates.	1					
		-Traceability using excel sheet or home grown tools but no plans or not enough data pointers available.	0					
		-No/Partial traceability.						
Do you have integrated view of the code promotion process from Dev to QA to Ops?	Dashboards	-Fully Integrated dashboard available for Dev to Ops using release management tools like ChaRM, "Transport Expresso"	4					
			3					
		-Partial view of code promotion process is available through tools like ChaRM, "Transport Expresso" (Not all features are used)	2					
		-Home grown tool or integrations of few open source tools which produces reports but most of it are status reports	1					

		not analysis reports	
		-Manual and person dependent way of reports and hence error prone.	0
		-No integrated view available	
How do you capture the deviations from the planned release calendar?	Dashboards	-Dashboards and reports produced from Devops tools like SolMan 7.2 focussed build showing clear deviations from the plans	4
		-Home grown tool or integrations of few open source tools which produces reports but most of it are status reports not analysis reports e.g. IBM detailed status entry in SolMan 7.1	3
			2
		-Plan and actual is tracked using some tool like MS project	1
		-Manual and person dependent way of reports and	0

| | | hence error prone -No dashboards and reports | | | | | |

D) Collaborative Development

Question	DevOps Capability	DevOps Score Guideline	Score	Actual score	Actual Finding	Does it business critical?	DevOps Recommendation
List down the configuration items (CI) under source control. List the criteria to identify it as a configuration item (CI).	Configuration Management	- Clear identification of CI and version system control is in place - Clear identification of CI but version system control is not in place for all - No clear identification of CI and no version system control is in place	4 2 0				

Is the software configuration management system integrated with development, test and deployment?	Configuration Management	- IDE, test stages, production, test management system are integrated with SCM system e.g. with Solman - No integration of any system with SCM system	4 0				
How are the baselines defined? What is the baseline strategy ? What is the branch / stream / trunk configuration ?	Configuration Management	- Definition in place for 'When and how baseline is created'; baseline is created in all stages in a continuous manner for all types of builds. - Baselines strategy is not defined; baseline is not practiced.	4 0				
How do you manage remotely located teams for effective delivery of the product? Explain the collaboration tools implemented if any.	Collaborative Development	- Teams are distributed geographically and work assignments are done through collaborative tools like JIRA, Solution Manager 7.2 focused build etc with real time visibility about the progress of the task	4				

		- Managed partially using other collaborative tools	2				
		- Managed manually	0				
How is work assigned and tracked ?	Collaborative Development	- Work is assigned and tracked through collaborative tools e.g. SolMan	4				
		- Work is assigned and tracked on excel sheets	2				
		- Work is assigned and tracked through emails	1				
		- Work is assigned and tracked verbally	0				
How is code review done ?	Collaborative Development	- Code reviews using code review tools integrated with build management process e.g. SCI+, CAST etc	4				
		- Code reviews using code review tools but not tightly integrated with build management	3				

		process e.g. SCI+, CAST etc	2					
		- Manual code review process and tracked in tool	1					
		- Manual code review process but no tracking	0					
		- No code review process						
How much do you test during development? Is there any built-in unit testing in place?	Collaborative Development	Manual Unit testing with 80 to 90% coverage based on functional specification	3					
		Manual Unit testing with coverage between 40 to 50% based on functional specification	2					
		Manual unit testing and depends on individual developers how much to test	1					
		There is no unit testing	0					
How is continuous integration achieved? How much of it is automated?	Build Management	- Continuous integration implemented code integration, build management, defect	4					

		management, configuration management, unit testing in automated way.	3					
		- Build automation and unit testing is achieved.	2					
		- Build automation is there but no unit test	1					
		- Both Build and unit testing manual	0					
		- Build is manual, no unit testing. No build and SCM integration						
Do you track build results? Is automated mail triggered	Build Management	- Build management tool in place, tracking of build log by dev team, log is sent automatically with key errors, dashboards, reports in place	4					
		- Log is generated but no dashboards reports but sent in mail	3					
		- Log is not captured but build failure or	2					

		success is just notified	1					
		- Log is tracked manually	0					
		- No automated way to track the log, log is not produced and sent to the stakeholders						
How is a release planned? User stories, prioritization, team velocity, release criteria.	Release Planning	- Done in an agile way. Continuously tracked and updated using tools like JIRA or SolMan	4					
		- Done in an agile way but loosely executed. Sometimes missed deadlines.	3					
		- Iterative planning but not agile planning. Resources have to be added in an adhoc manner based upon where the crunch is.	2					
		- Waterfall model. The big problems are uncovered quite late in the development cycle.	1 0					

		- Not much of a release planning. Frequently dates have to be changed or resources need to be added. Not much of visibility in terms of release dates.						
How are changes managed during development cycle ?	Change Management	- Using requirements management tool integrated with collaborative lifecycle tools e.g. using SOlMan 7.2.	4					
		- Using requirements management tool but no integration with collaborative lifecycle tools e.g. SolMan	3					
		- Managed and tracked using manual requirements management process	2					
		- Managed and tracked using separate Excel sheet which is not integrated with requirements management process	1					
			0					
		- Changes						

		managed over emails or verbally					
Are there dashboards and reports shown to monitor build, code review, unit testing results?	Dashboard, Traceability	- DevOps capability tools are used and dashboards and reports are displayed for build, code review, unit testing e. g. SolMan 7.2 with Focussed build	4				
		- Only build tool capability used to show dashboard and reports with complete traceability established manually	3				
		- Only build tool capability used to show dashboard and reports but there is no complete traceability	2				
		- Only build result logs are maintained but not in the form of reports or dashboards	1				
		- No Dashboard	0				

E) **Continuous Testing**

Question	DevOps Capability	DevOps Score Guideline	Score	Actual score	Actual Finding	Does it business critical?	DevOps Recommendation
In what stage of software lifecycle, test plan, test cases and test scripts are created?	Test Management and execution	- Test Cases, test plan & test scripts are written during high level design phase. - Before development - In parallel to development - Just before testing starts - No test documents	4 3 2 1 0				
Where are the test plan, test cases, test scripts stored?	Test Management and execution	- Usage of test management tool like HP ALM, worksoft, SolMan - In SCM tools with version control and baselines - In Repositories with no baseline or version control - Stored in local file system/testin	4 3 2 1 0				

		g boxes					
		- No test documents					
How often do you perform functional unit test?	Test Management and execution	- Continuous, Agile way	4				
		- Functional unit testing at end of each wave consisting of multiple sprints, Agile way	3				
		- All requirements are tested at the end of release, waterfall way	0				
Is it automated or manual testing? If automated then provide list of testing tools used.	Test Automation	- Fully automated testing and feedback mechanism, fully integrated CLM/ALM tools - Worksoft, SOlMan CBTA, HP UFT	4				
		- Partial automated functional testing not everything covered.	3				
		- Manual testing but using test management tool like Worksoft, HP	2				
			1				

		ALM, SolMan					
		- Manual testing and results recorded in defect tracking system	0				
		- Manual testing and defects in Spreadsheets.					
What are the various test environments?	Test Automation	- SIT-UAT-Preprod virtualized	4				
		- SIT-UAT-Preprod	3				
		- SIT-UAT but no Preprod	2				
		- SIT-UAT on same box	1				
		- Testing on developer's boxes	0				
How start of test execution in various phases communicated and monitored?	Traceability	-Automated communication with process hand offs and tracking of test status	4				
		- Automated communication from the tools with bigger distribution list but no dashboard, report tracking	3				
		- Automated	2				

		mail trigger from the build tool but no tracking	1				
		- Manual communication over the email.	0				
		- Verbal communication in meetings					
How do you monitor which build is deployed on test environment?	Traceability	- Release management process tracks the deployments automatically. Deployed build is tracked back and forth. Can be seen all the time in dashboard e.g. in Solution Manager dashboard	4				
			3				
		- Builds and environments are tracked using spreadsheet which are version controlled, and maintained in SCM repository.	2				
		- Builds and environments are tracked using spreadsheet and/or sent	1				

		over mail	0
		- Build deployments are communicated in mails	
		- Release management process doesn't exist	
Which tool is used for defect management? How are Defects captured and Tracked to closure ?	Traceability	- Defects are captured using tool like SOlMan, ALM, Worksoft with required metrics. This process is fully automated and changes are moved to next stage when all the defects are closed.	4
			3
		- Defects are captured using tool like SOlMan, ALM, Worksoft etc., without any metrics. Metrics are generated manually using spreadsheets with data from defect management tool.	2
			1
		- Defects are in spreadsheets	0

		but no metrics generated.					
		- Defects are individually captured by testers in spreadsheet.					
		- No tool or spreadsheet, defects are communicated over emails.					
How do you trace requirement to the test cases	Traceability	- Traceability using SolMan, HP ALM, Worksoft and / or integrating them	4				
		- Traceability using spreadsheet with metrics and dashboards	3				
		- Traceability in spreadsheet and no dashboards / metrics	2				
		- Traceability doesn't exist	1				
		- No traceability, no requirement management, no test management	0				
Does development	Test Data Management	- Yes, unit test cases are	4				

team share unit test cases and results for every test release?		automated and code coverage dashboard is available for all releases.	3				
		- Unit test cases are manually run by individual developer, a consolidated report is shared before every release.	2				
		- Unit test cases are run by individual developers no consolidated report available.	1				
		- Unit tests are partially run and when asked for, no formal unit test cases exists.	0				
		- Unit test are NOT run, and no unit test cases exists.					
How close is your testing environment's configuration to your production environment?	Test Data Management	- Test Environment (SIT/UAT/Pre-Prod) are identical to production environment, including hardware and software configuration.	4				
		- Test	2				

		environments (SIT/UAT/Pre-Prod) are partially identical to production environment, software configuration matches, but hardware does not.	1				
		- Test environments are similar in configuration but not identical	0				
		- Test environments are neither identical nor similar to production environment					
When are "Non Functional Test Requirements" (Smoke/ Performance) collected and when these Tests are carried out?	Test Automation	- Very early at the requirement/ design stage and modified during the development lifecycle. Tests carried out after unit test and at every test environment and are fully automated	4 3				
		- Very early at the requirement/ design stage and modified during the development lifecycle.					

		Tests carried out after unit test and at every test environment and are not fully automated	2				
		- Requirements are collected only during testing and tests are conducted at completion of functional testing and prior to deployment and are partially automated.	1				
		- Requirements are collected on adhoc basis and tests are conducted prior to deployment and may not be fully automated	0				
		- Adhoc/Need basis					
Who Provide/Creates test data sets and how close is it to Production data set?	Test Data Management	- Testing team creates own data set, in-line with production data set.	3				
		- Testing team creates own dataset,	2				

| | | not inline with production data.

- Testing is done on Ad-Hoc data set created by tester during testing. | 1 | | | | |

F) Continuous Release and Deployment

Question	DevOps Capability	DevOps Score Guideline	Score	Actual score	Actual Finding	Does it business critical?	DevOps Recommendation
List down the types of releases and time line of each type of release. Provide details of applications like names, technology. Provide separate document if project already maintaining it	Release Management	Incidents, defects, enhancements, projects, requirements with time line of each type of release.	NA				
Describe release management process for each type of application and release.	Release Management	- Release management using SolMan ChaRM, transport expresso and end to end traceability with well-	4				

		defined and tracking process by integrating it with other areas like requirement management and test management	3					
		- Release management using tools like SolMan ChaRM, transport expresso but no traceability till production.	2					
		- Release management using excel sheet with end to end traceability	1					
		- Manual release management process using excel sheet but no traceability with requirements	0					
		- No proper release management process						
How do you capture deviations	Release Management	- Tools like Solman 7.2 FB, JIRA are	3					

from the release calendar proactively and create feedback to bring it on track ?		used. Deviations are shown in reports in dynamic way. - Release calendar is tracked on regular basis and deviations are captured ahead of time. - Release calendar exists in excel sheet and deviations are discussed during status meeting - Reactive approach	2 1 0				
What are the contents of the release note which are shared with the operations team?	Release Management	- Release note is automatically derived from release tool like SOlMan Release Management FB - Release note is created in word or excel with build no, deployment instructions, environment details, story numbers	4 2 1				

		- Release note with deployment instructions are sent in mail with details decided by individual person	0				
		- No release note created and deployment instructions are sent over mail					
How do you track CI-Build Number-Release-Deployment environment?	Release Management	- Automatic tracking report generated using tools like SolMan 7.2 release management	4				
		- Tracking using excel sheet but manual effort	2				
		- No tracking	0				
How is environment provisioned (on premise, cloud based)?	Environment Management	- Cloud based	4				
		- On Premise	2				
How do you keep test environment and production environment in sync?	Environment Management	- Prod and UAT/SIT/REG environment are in sync from all respect	4				
			3				

		- Prod and regression test environment are in sync	2				
		- Configs & repository same - data different	0				
		- There is no predefined strategy. Environments are not kept same					
What is the time required to provide the environment?	Environment Management	- Cloud based and about 2 to 3 days	4				
		- Hosted environments so about 1 to 2 weeks	2				
		- Hosted environments so about 4 to 6 weeks	1				
Does environment availability need to be considered while doing release planning?	Environment Management	- Cloud based and environments available on demand so release planning does not need to consider env availability	4				
		- VM virtualization so release planning not	3				

		affected	2					
		- There is good coordination between Dev and Ops so manageable	1					
		- To some extent	0					
		- Yes, release planning is affected by environment availability						
How is deployment done currently? Is it manual, automated, using scripts?	Deployment Automation	- Automatic using DevOps tools like Urban Code or batch job using SolMan CharM or "Transport Expresso"	4					
		- Manual using tools like Urban Code, SolMan CharM or "Transport Expresso"	3					
		- Semi-automatic using manual + scripts	1					
		- Manual deployments	0					
What is deployment approval process with entry and	Deployment Automation	- Automatic process using release + deployment management	4					

exit criteria?		tools like SolMan and Incident Management tool for all environments	3					
		- Automatic process using release + deployment management tools like SolMan and Incident Management tool for all non-productive environments	2					
		- Semi-automatic process	0					
		- No approval process and manual collaboration						
In terms of governance how is auditing and reporting done on the releases performed to various environments.	Deployment Automation	- Automated auditing and report generation using application, automation deployment tools	4					
		- Manual generation of reports	2					
		- No auditing and reports	0					

G) **Continuous Monitoring**

Question	DevOps Capability	DevOps Score Guideline	Score	Actual score	Actual Finding	Does it business critical?	DevOps Recommendation
What are the performance thresholds defined and how are those monitored?	Monitor Capacity and Optimize	- Automated monitoring using tool like SolMan TechMon and OCC is in place	4				
		- Automated monitoring using tool like SolMan TechMon with thresholds defined.	3				
		- Thresholds defined and script based monitoring (e.g. by scheduling custom job, custom reports)	2				
		- No thresholds but proactive manual monitoring	1				
		- No thresholds defined and reactive approach.	0				
Is operations team involved from requirement analysis phase to give inputs about	Monitor capacity and optimize	- Operations team is involved actively in day to day planning meeting	4				
			3				

environments, deployments, capacity planning?		- Operations team is involved at the requirement baseline time and sought the inputs	2
		- Operations team is involved just to provide information of pipeline	1
		- Operations team is involved on adhoc basis	0
		- Operations team not involved in requirement analysis phase	
What is the timeline to increase the capacity of environment once threshold is reached?	Monitor Capacity and Optimize	- On demand within 2 hours	4
		- Less than a week	3
		- 2 to 4 weeks	2
		- 4 to 8 weeks	1
		- From 8 to 12 weeks	0
How do you monitor all the applications for errors, warnings, performance?	Monitoring performance and optimize	- Automated monitoring using tool like SolMan TechMon and automated feedback based on analysis through integration to incident management or notification	4
			3

		- Automated monitoring using tool like SolMan TechMon but no integration with incident management or notification	2					
		- Monitoring using scripts, custom reports, jobs etc	1					
		- Manual log monitoring answers communicating to respective teams concerned manually	0					
		- No monitoring						
How do you monitor environments for errors, warnings, performance?	Monitoring performance and optimize	- Automated monitoring using tool like SolMan TechMon and automated feedback based on analysis through integration to incident management or notification	4 3					
		- Automated monitoring using tool like SolMan TechMon but no integration with incident management or notification	2					

		- Monitoring using scripts, custom reports, jobs etc	1				
		- Manual log monitoring answer communicating to respective teams concerned manually	0				
		- No monitoring					
What are the tools used for monitoring?	Monitoring performance and optimize	- SolMan TechMon integrated to incident management or notification	4				
		- SolMan TechMon	3				
		- Scripts, custom reports, jobs etc	2				
		- Excel, Word etc	1				
		- No monitoring	0				
Are feedback tools and development tools integrated to maintain traceability from operations to developments?	Monitoring performance and optimize	- Tools used like SolMan ITSM, SNOW	4				
		- No integration of tools	0				
Is there any analytics, trend, report produced to create	Operational Analytics	- SolMan Dashboard & Analytics used	4				
		- Script based	2				

feedback for development team?		alert generation but no analytics	1				
		- Manual data feed and report creation	0				
		- No reports					
What is the process for event and incident management?	Event and Incident Management	- Incident management is done using DevOps tools like SolMan ITSM and integrated with release and dev process	4				
		- Incident management using tools like Remedy, CQ and manually integrated with release and dev process	3				
		- Incident management using tools like Remedy, CQ but not integrated with release process	2				
		- Incidents are communicated over mail by customer and logged in to excel sheet manually	1				
		- No incident management process	0				
What is the process for Capacity Planning?	Monitor Capacity and Optimize	- Using Latest Capacity Management Tools like	4				

		RCA tool of SolMan to monitor current trend and predict the timeline when we will run out of capacity, so that we can be proactive.	3				
		- Using Scripts to gather historical data and predict the timeline using excel graphs when we can run out of capacity.	0				
		- No Procedure					
Autoscaling	Monitor Capacity and Optimize	- Auto scaling configured to scale out and scale down the infrastructure/instances based on the configurable parameters (CPU, memory or message bus mechanisms)	4 3				
		- Scale out and Scale down is done manually after getting the threshold parameters.	2				
		- No room for scale out. Infrastructure need to be deployed.	0				
		- Application cannot scale					
High	Monitor	- Application	4				

Availability (HA) / Business Continuity	User Experience and Optimize	is configured for HA based on configurable parameters (performance, network outage). Failback is automated with "Zero Data Loss".	3				
		- Application is configured for HA based on configurable parameters (performance, network outage). Failback is manual with "Zero Data Loss".	2				
		- Application is configured for HA based on configurable parameters (performance, network outage). Failback is manual with agreed transactions loss. (Recovery point objective)	0				
		- Application is not configured for HA					

H) Continuous feedback

Question	DevOps Capability	DevOps Score Guideline	Score	Actual score	Actual Finding	Does it business critical?	DevOps Recommendation
How do you capture user feedback ?	User Feedback & Optimization	- Modern DevOps process like linking online errors, suggestions in the feedback tool with continuous business planning processes e.g. SolMan ITSM	4				
		- Tools like Remedy, SNOW are used for collecting online customer feedback	3				
		- Excel sheet is used with history tracking	2				
		- User feedback is communicated using mail via stakeholders	1				
		- There is no formal	0				

		process. User feedback is conveyed by customer to the management team					
What are the tools used for feedback collections?	User Feedback & Optimization	- Integrated online feedback collection service using Solman, ITSM - Tools like Remedy, SNOW, CQ used in isolation from end user - Excel sheet with history tracked in the form of incident versions - Excel based manually maintained - Incident managed using mail communication	4 3 2 1 0				
When is feedback captured?	User Feedback & Optimization	- Option to provide feedback anytime during all stages. - During crisis, post deployment, testing and development. - During crisis, post	4 3 2				

		deployment and testing	1					
		- Only during crisis and post deployment.	0					
		- Only when there is issue/crisis.						
How is user feedback analysed and optimized for continuous improvement?	User Feedback & Optimization	- Using DevOps analytics tools like "SmartCloud Analytics - Log Analysis " and optimizing feedback for continuous improvement	4					
		- Using standard reports from feedback tools and optimizing the outcome	3					
			2					
		- Techniques like RCA, interviewing, metrics, date filters are used	1					
		- Team discussions based on excel sheet date	0					
		- No optimization for continuous improvement						
How are pain points from feedback converted into action items?	User Feedback & Optimization	- Using some modern DevOps tools like SolMan ALM, integrated with continuous	4					

213

		business planning.	2				
		- Using excel sheets	0				
		- No action taken					
How is SLA being tracked?	User Feedback & Optimization	- Using some modern DevOps tools like ALM, integrated with continuous business planning.	4				
		- Using tools like Remedy, ServiceNow	3				
		- No tracking	0				
Is the Cross Team Feedback Mechanism in place? How is it practised?	User Feedback & Optimization	- Feedbacks are shared during shake hands for releases and tracked using standard mechanism	4				
		- Feedbacks are shared during shake hands for releases but not being tracked	3				
		- Feedbacks are shared periodically	2				
		- Feedbacks are shared only when issues occurs only	1				
		- Feedbacks are not shared	0				

I) Maturity Score

At last it will give us cummulatative actual maturity score based on our actual score.

J) Charts

At last it will show us DevOps maturity diagram based on our actual score.

NOTES

NOTES

14.0 . GIT – Tips & Tricks

What is GIT?
- Distributed Version Control System (DVCS)
- Created by Linus Torvalds.

GIT Client & Server Tools

Git Client Tools: CLI, SourceTree, GITHUB desktop, GITGUI, Eclipse, Microsoft Visual Studio

GIT Server Tools: GITHUB, Bitbucket, GITLAB

Setting Up GIT

Download - https://git-scm.com/downloads
Setting Up GIT
git config —global user.name 'sudipta'
git config —global user.email 'sudipta@booleanminds.com' git config -l

GIT Config

- Global Level
- System Level
- Repository Level.

GIT – Sample pseudo commands

- git cat-file -t <hash>
- git cat-file -p <hash>
- git cat-file -p <treehash>
- git cat-file -p <blobhash>

- **Config**
  - git config -l
  - git config --global --replace-all user.email 'parvezmisarwala@gmail.com'

- git config - -global core.autocrlf true (in case of windows)
- git config - -global core.autocrlf input (in case of mac and linux)
- git config - -global core.autocrlf false (if only windows)
- git config --global core.editor vim
- git config core-sparsecheckout true (to checkout selected directory). Details below
- git config - -global merge.tool kdiff3 (brew install kdiff3)
- git mergetool -t kdiff3
- git config - -global diff.tool kdiff3
- git config --global core.whitespace -trailing-space,-space-before-tab - This will disable whitespace warnings
- git config - -global clean.requireForce false

- **add, commit, amend**
    - git add .
    - git add -u - Stages only modified files and ignores untracked files
    - git add -i (for interactive staging)
    - git add file1.txt file2.txt file3.txt
    - git add *.txt
    - git add p
    - git rm —cached - To unstage
    - git reset HEAD <filename> - remove from staging
    - git commit
    - git commit -m <commit message>
    - git commit -am <commit message>
    - git commit - -amend
    - Exercise
        - 1. Create 4 files and commit these files in all separate commits
- Status
    - git status -u - Shows untracked files
    - git status -sb - Gives output in short format of your branch
- **.gitignore**
    - .gitignore - to share the ignore files
    - exclude - for local ignore

- git check-ignore -v * - To list ignored files

- **status**
  - git status
  - git status -u : shows untracked files
  - git status -sb : gives output in short format of your branch

- **log**
  - git shortlog -s -n : To get the number of commits
  - git log -p
  - git log - -oneline
  - git log - -graph
  - git log --oneline --abbrev-commit --all --graph
  - git log - -stat: In each commit shows statistics for files modified
  - git log - -shortstat: From the --stat command.git displays only the changed/ insertions/deletions line
  - git log - -name-only: After the commit information shows the list of files modified.
  - git log - -name-status: Display the list of files affected with added/modified/deleted information as well.
  - git log --pretty=oneline
    - %H-Commit hash, %h-Abbreviated Commit hash
    - %T- Tree hash, %t-Abbreviated tree hash
    - %P-Parent hashes, %p-Abb.. parent hashes
    - %an-Author name, %ae-Author email, %ad-Author date, %ar-Author date relative
    - %cn-committer name, %ce-Committer email, %cd-Committer date, %cr-Relatives
    - %s: Subject (commit message)

- **Alias**
  - git config —global alias.co commit
  - git config —globbal alias.last 'log -1 HEAD'
  - git config --global alias.unstage 'reset HEAD —'

- **rm**
  - git rm - Remove files from the working tree and from the index
  - -q, --quiet   do not list removed files
  - --cached   only remove from the index (to untrack)
  - -n, --dry-run   dry run
  - -f, --force   override the up-to-date check
  - -r   allow recursive removal
  - --ignore-unmatch   exit with a zero status even if nothing matched

- **mv**
- manually renaming a file
- **clean** - Remove untracked file from working directory
  - git clean -f -n - Show what will be deleted with the -n option:
  - git clean -f -d - Also removes directories
  - git clean -f -X - Also removes ignored files
  - git clean -f -x - Removes both ignored and non-ignored files
  - git clean -i

- Revert - To undo a committed snap shop
- Reset - Reset Current head to specified state
  - Git reset --hard
    - Clean directory, no modified files
    - Modified files, not staged yet
    - Staged file, not committed yet
  - Git Reset --soft - Does not touch the index file or the working tree at all
    - Clean directory, no modified files
    - Modified files, not staged yet
    - Staged file, not committed yet
  - Git Reset - -mixed -Resets the index but not the working tree
    - Clean directory, no modified files
    - Modified files, not staged yet
    - Staged file, not committed yet

- branch, merge, rebase, rebase -i, conflict, mergetool
    - View conflicted files
        - git diff --name-only —diff-filter=U
        - git ls-files -u | awk '{print $4}' | sort | uniq
        - git ls-files -u | cut -f 2 | sort -u
    - View if branch is merged or unmarked
        - git branch --merged master
        - git branch --no-merged master
    - Rebase
        - git rebase master
        - git rebase —onto
            - git rebase --onto master next topic
            - git rebase --onto topicA~5 topicA~3 topicA
        - git rebase -i
- **Patch**
    - git format-patch master --stdout > fix_empty_poster.patch : This will create a new file fix_empty_poster.patch with all changes from the current (fix_empty_poster) against master.
    - git apply --stat fix_empty_poster.patch: This will show commits which is present in path file
    - git am --signoff < fix_empty_poster.patch - This will apply the patch
    - git format-patch -10 HEAD --stdout > 0001-last-10-commits.patch: The last 10 patches from head in a single patch file:
    - git format-patch -1 <sha> --stdout > specific_commit.patch: To generate patch from a specific commit (not the last commit):
    - Apply Patch
        - Checkout to a new branch: $ git checkout review-new-feature
        - # If you received the patch in a single patch file: $ cat new-feature.patch | git am
        - # If you received multiple patch files: $ cat *.patch | git am

- cherrypick
    - To pick up a particular commit

- Stash
- remote

- git remote
- git remote -v
- git remote show origin
- git remote rename pb paul
- git remote rm paul
- git branch --set-upstream-to=upstream/foo foo
- Clone
- Sync Repository with Pull Push fetch merge and rebase
  - Pull - Updates the working directory

- Fetch and Merge
- tag
  - git tag v1.0 -m 'tag message'
  - git tag -l
  - git checkout v1.0 -b NewBranch

- submodules
  - A submodule allows you to keep another Git repository in a subdirectory of your repository.
  - Submodule does not automatically upgrade
  - The other repository has its own history, which does not interfere with the history of the current repository. This can be used to have external dependencies such as third party libraries for example.
    - git submodule add https://github.com/pmisarwala/myrepo1.git
    - cat .gitmodules
    - Clone a repo with submodule
      - git submodule update - -init
- **subtree**
  - Add a subtree: git subtree add --prefix .vim/bundle/fireplace https://github.com/tpope/vim-fireplace.git master —squash
  - To update: git subtree pull --prefix .vim/bundle/fireplace https://github.com/tpope/vim-fireplace.git master --squash
- **Split** repository

- git subtree split --prefix=lib -b split
- **symlinks**
  - ln -s originalfile linkedfile
  - git ls-files -s
  - git config - -system core.symlinks true

- **show**
  - git show <commit ID>: filename - This will show content of file for a particular commit
- help -a
- annotate, blame, br, ci
- citool, describe difftool
- Hooks

To Amend Last commit
- One method
    - git rebase —interactive '31f73c0^'
    - choose edit instead of default pick
    - make changes and do git add .
    - git rebase —continue
    - (This will update the current commit, but commit ID will be new)
- Second method (
    - make changes and do git add .
    - git commit —all —amend
- Third method
    - git rebase -i <commit ID> (edit)
    - update the contents..
    - git add .
    - git commit —amend
    - git rebase —continue
- Fourth Option
    - git reset HEAD~
    - git add ...

- git commit -c ORIG_HEAD

Visual Studio
- Git cherry-pick is supported in MS Visual Studio 2015 Update-2
- Submodules are supported in MS VS 2015 Update-2

Bitbucket Plugin Development

- Install Atlassian Plugin SDK
- Run command atlas-create-stash-plugin
    - com.atlassian.stash.plugin.demoplugin
    - demo-plugin
- Run command atlas-create-stash-plugin-module
    - 8
    - Democlass

NOTES

NOTES

NOTES

15.0. Test your knowledge

1. Mention most common challenges faced by your scrum teams.

2. In Agile, is it fair for a customer to ask for expected completion date for a new work item (user story)?

3. Do we accept changes within a sprint, or not? If we do, won't it disrupt our sprint plan that is in progress? And, if we don't, would we be less of an 'agile' team?

4. Mention Kanban myths and misconceptions.

5. Mention Agile myths and misconceptions.

6. What are the common Agile mistakes?

7. What are the common KANBAN mistakes?

8. How do you decide the sprint length for a team?

9. In Agile what are the common estimation techniques?

10. How many planning you are doing in SCRUM?

NOTES

NOTES

NOTES

NOTES

Printed in Great Britain
by Amazon